THE OFFICIAL ITV F1 SPORT GRAND PRIX GUIDE 2000

THIS IS A CARLTON BOOK

CLD21628

This edition published in 2000 for
Colour Library Direct Ltd
New Mill
New Mill Lane
Witney
Oxon OX8 5TF

10 9 8 7 6 5 4 3 2 1

A CIP catalogue record for this book is
available from the British Library

The publisher has taken reasonable steps to
check the accuracy of the facts contained
herein at the time of going to press but can
take no responsibility for any errors

ISBN 1 84222 009 8

Project Editor: Chris Hawkes
Project Art Direction: Paul Oakley
Production: Sarah Corteel
Picture Research: Debora Fioravanti

Printed and bound in Great Britain by
Butler & Tanner Ltd, Frome and London

THE OFFICIAL
ITV F1 SPORT GRAND PRIX GUIDE 2000

Bruce Jones

Colour Library Direct

F1 CONTENTS

Chapter 3

Chapter 4

Chapter 5

8

MURRAY WALKER

Grand Prix years don't come much better than 1999 but, in my ever optimistic way, I really do think that the first Formula One season of the new millennium will have even more to savour. The last year of the twentieth century gave us an exciting mix of drama and ever-changing fortunes. It featured the elimination halfway through the season of the driver generally acknowledged to be the best in the world; a battle for the two championships which went right down to the last race; and dubious political moves which tarnished the sport's image. But it all came out right in the end – with Mika Hakkinen a very worthy drivers' champion and Ferrari the top constructor. Now, looking ahead, there are glittering prospects for 2000.

In Japan, with a drive of stunning brilliance under enormous pressure, Hakkinen, the self-styled "Flying Finn", became only the seventh driver in history to win two successive championships. On a gigantic high and in a brand new McLaren–Mercedes-Benz, his target for 2000 will be to become only the second man ever to do the hat-trick. The immortal five-times champion Juan Manuel Fangio was the first but, good as Mika is, I'll be very surprised if he can join the great Argentinian.

The year 2000 is going to be all about ability, reliability and consistency. We won't know who has got the best blend until the season is well under way, but there are several likely contenders. It was a lack of reliability and consistency that cost McLaren the Constructors' title in '99 and great strength in both areas that enabled Ferrari to succeed. After a six-day race lay-off Michael Schumacher showed in Malaysia and Japan that he had lost none of his consummate ability, and his burning ambition to become Ferrari's first world champion since 1979 will be undiminished. Will Ferrari new boy, the talented Brazilian Rubens Barrichello, be able to challenge his new superstar team-mate for the title? I think not, but I can see him winning races. Hakkinen's McLaren partner David Coulthard? Races yes, but the title no. Not against Hakkinen and Schumacher.

What of the rest? Two teams in particular should be right up there: Jordan and Jaguar. Jordan's Heinz-Harald Frentzen was the revelation of 1999 after his transfer from Williams. He took the chequered flag twice and could have won more races but for bad luck. A possible contender for the championship at one point, he should be even more of a threat in 2000 after a season's experience with his ever-improving team. Jaguar, the renamed Stewart team, should be up at the front, too. It takes a long time to build a winning team, but Stewart did it in only three years (it took Jordan eight) and now, bankrolled by Ford and with a hungry Eddie Irvine eager to prove that he can beat the rest, they just might make it into the McLaren/Ferrari bracket. Finally, in spite of the fact that I got it very wrong last year by prophesying success for the new BAR team, I'm going to do it again. Now with Honda power and the team's first year of bitterly won operational experience behind him, the brilliant Jacques Villeneuve, world champion of 1997, could be a winner again. And wouldn't it be marvellous if he was!

But that's not all. There are going to be a lot of other new situations to intrigue us. Williams with BMW power to propel the gigantically talented Ralf Schumacher. The gifted Italian Jarno Trulli partnering Heinz-Harald Frentzen at Jordan. Johnny Herbert out to show us all he can beat his Jaguar team-mate Eddie Irvine. A desperately needed new car from Benetton for Giancarlo Fisichella and Alexander Wurz. Jean Alesi and newcomer Nick Heidfeld at Prost. Strong packages from Sauber, Arrows and Minardi. But, sadly, no Damon Hill, for the first time since 1991. A great champion who wisely decided to call it a day when he felt the time had come to move on. No one will miss him more than I will.

The good news, though, is that what I confidently expect to be a great year will be even better on ITV as a result of a new contract with Formula One. More on-car cameras and a lot of exciting plans for improved coverage of the sport. So get ready for another great season of F1 viewing. Everything you need to know is in this *Grand Prix Guide*. Like I always say, Formula One gets better all the time!

ANALYSIS OF THE 2000 GRAND PRIX SEASON

One of the beauties of Formula One is the sheer variety of venues visited. It's not like football in which a pitch is a pitch and the main change from venue to venue for the players is the quality of the changing rooms, and the main difference to the fans is the quality of the grandstands. Ask a Formula One driver if all Grand Prix circuits are the same and the answer will be a definite 'no'. They are all different. And thank goodness for that, as all fans will echo their approval of the fact that each Grand Prix offers a distinctive flavour and challenge of its own.

The Teams

Who will win the first Formula One World Championship of the 21st century? That is the question.

I'm sure that many of you will have firm ideas on this. And I'm equally sure that all but the most optimistic of you will reckon that the driver will come from either the McLaren or Ferrari camp, with one or other of those teams coming away with the Constructors Cup. Indeed, the weight of evidence supporting your thinking is strong and with no changes in regulations for the 2000 season there's no real reason to expect any major changes in the balance of power. In addition, with both teams offering broadly the same chassis/engine packages, very little has changed in their camps, save for the fact that Ferrari has traded in one number two driver, Eddie Irvine, for another, Rubens Barrichello.

Certainly, Ferrari won't be planning for its number one driver, Michael Schumacher, to miss six mid-season Grands Prix with a broken leg again. So they should fare better and perhaps clinch their first drivers' championship since Jody Scheckter took the title in 1979. But, then again, McLaren won't be looking to throw away as many points as they did in 1999 with their litany of mechanical and professional failures. So, come what may, it should be another epic season between the sport's two top teams.

However, what of the rest? There appears to be a new world order shaping up in their wake, with Jordan scaling new heights by comfortably placing third overall last year, while Stewart also moved to new heights by ranking fourth in its third and final season before being taken over by Ford and renamed Jaguar Racing. There is no reason why they shouldn't maintain this form. Jordan will simply be

McLAREN FERRARI JORDAN WILLIAMS JAGUAR BE

GOING FOR GOLD: Michael Schumacher will be going all-out for his third title and, most importantly, his first for Ferrari

looking for more of the same from Heinz-Harald Frentzen, a driver that many said was the best last year as he won twice and placed third overall. His new team-mate, Jarno Trulli, is sure to attack the races with more gusto than the retiring Damon Hill did last year. In Jaguar's case, the arrival of Irvine from Ferrari should boost the team now that he's got a taste both for winning and for not being a number two driver any more. But Johnny Herbert won't be looking to lie down and play a supportive role.

All motorsport is cyclical and this is why it's hard to imagine Williams staying down the order for long. Yet the former champions may not be heading back to the sharp end of the field for a year or more, unless the new works BMW engine proves competitive from the outset. You can be sure that Ralf

Schumacher – another star of the 1999 campaign – will give it his all, matching his new-found consistency with his undoubted speed. However, for the team not to slide down the order, they need to have a driver racing hard in the number two seat.

On the subject of engines, British American Racing pulled off a coup by landing works Honda engines for its second season. Indeed, this was the sum total of its achievements after its first season saw it score not a single point despite Jacques Villeneuve's Herculean efforts. The team will even be receiving engines one grade better than the Honda engines Jordan will be using. So, if the team doesn't progress in its second year, it won't be the engines that let it down.

Benetton appears to be on a slide, as their cars were last year, and with no

change on the engine or driver front, it's going to be down to the designers to find some grip. Fortunately, engine supplier Supertec has promised more horsepower for 2000. This will also be welcomed by the other teams using the French engines, namely Arrows, as it continues its fight with Minardi not to be last.

Two teams that will be desperate to move forward are Prost and Sauber, with the former team showing good form both at the Nurburgring last year and then again at Suzuka. If Peugeot can improve its engine, Jean Alesi and Formula 3000 champion Nick Heidfeld could make boss Alain Prost smile. Sauber is at a low ebb, but the incoming Mika Salo will be delighted to be reunited with the Ferrari engines that he enjoyed for six races last year, even if the car beneath him is no longer Ferrari red.

ETTON SAUBER PROST ARROWS B.A.R. MINARDI

McLAREN

LOOKING FOR RELIABILITY

F1

McLaren had all the speed it needed in 1999, but not the reliability. If the team finds this for the 2000 season, then Mika Hakkinen and David Coulthard will have a fantastic year.

Last year proved an unnecessarily trying year for McLaren. And this was not something that you would have predicted had you seen the team's form at the opening round in Melbourne where Mika Hakkinen and David Coulthard qualified on the front row by a huge margin and then blasted off to open out a massive gap at the front. Better still, Michael

Schumacher had had to start the re-started race from the rear of the grid. Yet, both cars were to fail and McLaren came away with nothing. This fragility was to plague them through the first half of the season, with Coulthard retiring from three of the first four races.

The speed of the McLaren/Mercedes/Hakkinen combination was always impressive,

THE VIPs

Ron Dennis

Ron has worked his way from mechanic to be boss of the most professional team in Formula One after rising up the ladder with his Rondel Formula Two team. Took over McLaren in 1980 and has since guided the team to seven Constructors' Cups and initiated the world-beating McLaren F1 sportscar project. He never stops.

Adrian Newey

This is the designer that all the Formula One teams want to employ, as he has been the class leader in aerodynamics for most of the 1990s. Joined McLaren from Williams in 1997 after a hugely successful spell there, but had shone before that with the Leyton House team.

THINKING TO VICTORY: McLaren boss Ron Dennis is deep in thought as he tries to work out the best way for his drivers to put one over Ferrari

FOR THE RECORD

Country of origin: . . . . .England
Team base: . . . . .Woking, England
Date of formation: 1963
Active years in Formula One: . . . . .From 1964
Grands Prix contested: 492
Wins: 123
Pole positions: 103
Fastest laps: 88
Constructors' Cup victories: 1974, 1984, 1985, 1988,
. . . . 1989, 1990, 1991, 1998

Drivers and Results 1999

Driver	Nationality	Races	Wins	Pts	Pos
Mika Hakkinen	Finnish	16	5	76	1st
David Coulthard	Scottish	16	2	48	4th

Car specifications

Sponsors: . . . . .West, Mercedes, Mobil, Boss, TAG-Heuer
Team principal: . . . . .Ron Dennis
Team manager: . . . . .David Ryan
Designer: . . . . .Adrian Newey
Chief engineer: . . . . .Steve Hallam
Test driver: . . . . .Olivier Panis
Chassis: . . . . .McLaren MP4-15
Engine: . . . . .Mercedes V10

THE BRAIN OF FORMULA ONE: Adrian Newey is the designer all designers look up to. And McLaren will be hoping that he has produced the best chassis again

The year ahead

One thing that is clear looking at 2000 is that McLaren boss Ron Dennis is not interested in adopting Ferrari's preferred policy of team orders. For Dennis, a team should never have a number one driver and a number two.

For that, Coulthard will be grateful, as he usually was just that fraction slower than Hakkinen. Their equipment will be top rate again, with Adrian Newey expected to design the class-leading chassis. Mercedes will be looking for yet more horsepower from their engines. And, as shown at Suzuka, McLaren has found the ability to call the shots in the pitlane as well and no longer need fear Ferrari's often race-turning strategy decisions.

An illustrious past

Bruce McLaren would have had no idea what a major player in the sport his team would become when he founded it in 1963. Sadly, the main success it achieved was in the CanAm sportscar series, although Bruce won two Grands Prix in his own cars before his death in 1970. The team was kept going and was rewarded with Emerson Fittipaldi winning the 1974 world title and then James Hunt doing likewise two years later.

Dennis took the marque over in 1980 and McLaren had a great period in the mid-1980s as Niki Lauda and Alain Prost won titles, with Ayrton Senna emulating them in the early 1990s. However, it was only in 1997 that the team started winning again for the first time since 1993. However, that year proved to be Jacques Villeneuve's year for Williams, as Coulthard won only once more, at Monza, then Hakkinen scored his first win in the season's finale at Jerez.

McLaren's form was almost other worldly at the start of 1998 as Hakkinen won the Australian opener from Coulthard. Hakkinen then won again in Brazil. And the rest could do nothing about it. Ferrari, with the assistance of Goodyear, fought back, with Michael Schumacher winning three races in a row mid-season to stay in touch. However, Hakkinen won the last two races to bring his tally to eight wins to be sure of his first world title. And, with Coulthard winning once and finishing second six times, the Constructors' Cup was theirs as well.

as the Finn qualified on pole in 11 of the first 13 races, with Coulthard seldom far behind, and so Hakkinen should have waltzed to a second title in a row. Sure, he threw away a victory by crashing out of the lead at Imola, but there were mistakes that cost him dear. Such as losing a wheel at Silverstone, being spun out of the lead by his own team-mate at the A1-Ring and then having a blow-out at Hockenheim. Then, with Irvine pushing him hard on points if seldom on the track, he perhaps had reason to curse McLaren's equitable approach when Coulthard led all the way and didn't cede to him at Spa. But noone other than Mika can be held responsible for him spinning out of the lead at Monza.

That the title went to the final round is a travesty, but Mika's form was such at Suzuka that he won the race and with it the crown, with rival Irvine nowhere in sight. However, everyone was left with the impression that McLaren must stop making silly mistakes, while Mika should stop spinning off on Ferrari's home ground.

Coulthard refused to play the number two role, quite rightly. Not that the team asked to him to until the final two Grands Prix. And he added victories in the British and Belgian GPs to his tally. He should have won too at Magny-Cours but his car broke, and then at the Nurburgring, but he pressed too hard in the wet and fell off.

MIKA HAKKINEN

GOING FOR A THIRD

Nationality: . . . . .FINNISH
Born: . . . . . . .SEPTEMBER 28, 1968,
. . . . .HELSINKI, FINLAND
Teams: . . . . .LOTUS 1991-1992,
. . . . .MCLAREN 1993-2000

Career record

First Grand Prix: .1991 UNITED STATES
GP Starts: 128
Wins: .14
(1997 European GP, 1998 Australian GP,
1998 Brazilian GP, 1998 Spanish GP,
1998 Monaco GP, 1998 Austrian GP,
1998 German GP, 1998 Luxembourg GP,
1998 Japanese GP, 1999 Brazilian GP,
1999 Spanish GP, 1999 Canadian GP,
1999 Hungarian GP, 1999 Japanese GP)
Pole positions: 21
Fastest laps: 13
Points: 294
Honours: . . . . . .1999 & 1998 WORLD
CHAMPION, 1990 BRITISH FORMULA
THREE CHAMPION, 1988 EUROPEAN
FORMULA OPEL CHAMPION, 1987
SCANDINAVIAN FORMULA FORD
CHAMPION, 1986 FINNISH
KARTING CHAMPION

Mika Hakkinen was really made to work for his second world title last year, and that has made him even more focused on adding a third this year, and doing so before the final round.

At the end of 1997, Mika Hakkinen scored his long overdue first Grand Prix win. It was handed to him by Jacques Villeneuve. But it was a win. At the end of 1998, he won the Japanese GP and with it his first world title. Then, at the end of 1999, he again won the Japanese GP, and with it his second world title. But it had been a draining fight that forced Mika to experience every emotion possible. It should be said, though, that frustration must have been the one he experienced most.

When Mika qualified on pole at Melbourne by half a second from team-mate David Coulthard, with Michael Schumacher's Ferrari a further 0.8s in arrears, he must have thought that it was going to be McLarens all the way in 1999. But neither he nor Coulthard finished, and Eddie Irvine was a surprise winner for Ferrari. Everyone can afford a bad result, but it wasn't to be the last...

Consider the fact that Mika put his car on pole 11 times, but turned only three of these into wins, as well as winning twice when he wasn't on pole, and you will understand that things didn't run to plan. He crashed out of the lead at Imola and Monza, lost a wheel at Silverstone, was spun from the lead by Coulthard at the A1-Ring and had a blow-out at Hockenheim. But, just when it looked as though Irvine would beat him to the title, Mika won at Suzuka. However, it was a year that revealed more of his emotion than ever before.

He will be yet stronger for all of this, though. In fact, Mika is already talking of making it three titles in a row, believing that McLaren and Mercedes will provide him with the equipment to beat all others.

A champion in everything

Mika starred in karting before taking a clean sweep of the Finnish, Swedish and Nordic Formula Ford titles in 1987.

A MAN IN CONTROL: Mika Hakkinen had a troubled 1999, but when matters outside his control don't trip him up, he is the man to beat. Will he make it three in a row?

Formula Opel Euroseries Champion in 1988, he won the British Formula Three title in 1990. He then jumped direct to Formula One with Lotus in 1991 and showed immediate pace. But Lotus was a team in decline and mentor Keke Rosberg guided him to McLaren in 1993, when a gamble that Ayrton Senna wouldn't return went wrong. However, Mika replaced Michael Andretti three races before the end of the year and immediately outqualified the great Brazilian.

McLaren wasn't as it is now and it took years of showing promise before the team rediscovered its winning touch in 1997, two years after his life-threatening accident at Adelaide. Since then, Mika has reminded everyone why he was the pick of the crop in the junior formulae.

DAVID COULTHARD

KEEPING UP WITH MIKA

David Coulthard has lost out to McLaren team-mate Mika Hakkinen in both the 1998 and 1999 title races. This year he wants to take the lead.

Nationality: . . . . .SCOTTISH
Born: . . . . .MARCH 27, 1971,
. . . . .TWYNHOLM, SCOTLAND
Teams: . . . . . .WILLIAMS 1994-1995,
. . . . .MCLAREN 1996-2000

Career record

First Grand Prix: . . .1994 SPANISH GP
Starts: .90
Wins: 6
*(1995 Portuguese GP, 1997 Australian GP,
1997 Italian GP, 1998 San Marino GP,
1999 British GP, 1999 Belgian GP)*
Pole positions: 8
Fastest laps: 11
Points: 221
Honours: . . .1991 BRITISH FORMULA
THREE RUNNER-UP & WINNER OF
MACAU GP, 1989 MCLAREN
AUTOSPORT YOUNG DRIVER OF THE
YEAR, 1988 SCOTTISH KART CHAMPION

GETTING EVEN: David Coulthard reckons that 2000 could be his season and is confident that he can take the fight to team-mate Hakkinen in the battle for the title

A winner all the way

To understand the challenge facing David Coulthard in his fifth year with McLaren one needs to understand his last two seasons in particular, seasons in which his team-mate Mika Hakkinen has not only assumed the role of team leader, but also raced to two world titles. Indeed, in the 32 Grands Prix in this period, Mika has won 13 and David three. And the statistics from qualifying are even more in the Finn's favour.

The crux, though, is that David has the speed, and the margin is often negligible or even in his favour. Yet, on other days, Hakkinen is in another class, such as in last year's Italian Grand Prix. So the question is whether David can raise his game for every race and maintain his concentration. After all, he must smart at the thought of pitching Hakkinen into a spin on the

first lap at the A1-Ring and the fact that he threw away victory at the Nurburgring. Indeed, had he not slid off in the wet when leading, he would have remained in the title race and not had to play a supporting role in the final two races of the year. And, had he not had to do so, he wouldn't have had to hang back to keep Eddie Irvine occupied at Suzuka or attempt to slow Michael Schumacher, matters that are at odds with a man of David's fair nature.

If there was bad luck going in the first half of 1999 at McLaren, most of it fell on David, with his mechanical failure when well clear in the French Grand Prix particularly unkind. However, he scored one more win that he'd managed in 1998, by winning both the British and Belgian Grands Prix, the latter after asserting his control over Hakkinen at the start.

A star in karting circles, David burst onto the Formula Ford scene in 1989. Second to Rubens Barrichello in the 1991 British Formula Three series, he won the prestigious Macau street race. Then, despite winning once in Formula 3000 in 1993, his career lost momentum. However, his test driver's role at Williams became a race ride on Ayrton Senna's death in 1994. David's first win followed in 1995, but he moved on to McLaren in 1996 as the team was finding its way with Mercedes and gave the combination its first win at Melbourne in the 1997 season-opener. He won again that year at Monza, but it was a Williams-dominated year. With McLaren finding the upper hand for 1998, that should have been a great year, but he won only at Imola and ended up third overall behind Hakkinen and Ferrari's Michael Schumacher.

FERRARI

IT'S NOW OR NEVER

Ferrari showed great strength throughout last season and pipped McLaren to the Constructors' Cup. However, the title that will give them universal prestige is the drivers' title, so this has to be their target in 2000.

THE VIPs

Jean Todt

This man has led teams to success in every one of the sport's top disciplines, namely Formula One, sportscars and rallying. He brought new discipline to Ferrari when he joined in 1993, something he had to have as a top rally co-driver before he became head of Peugeot Talbot Sport and led it to numerous wins in sportscars, rallies and desert raids.

Ross Brawn

Ross started his career at Williams, then worked at Force, Arrows and on the Jaguar sportscar project before joining Benetton. He is the master tactician, as shown when he guided Michael Schumacher to two World Championship titles at Benetton. He followed the German to Ferrari in 1997 and almost guided him to a third world title in 1997 and again in 1998.

Armed with a seemingly unlimited budget, top-ranking engines and enviable reliability, Ferrari should be a sure bet to race to another Constructors' Cup win in 2000, especially with Michael Schumacher back to full fitness. Faithful number two turned oh-so-nearly successful number one Eddie Irvine has departed for number one status at Jaguar Racing, swapping seats with Rubens Barrichello, so points should be plentiful from both drivers. However, the question remains whether they will be good enough to put one over McLaren, or was 1999 an aberration from the men from Woking who appeared to have the better car-engine package and yet contrived to throw points away almost as fast as they scored them last year?

When Enzo Ferrari ruled at Maranello, he professed to have no interest in the drivers' title. The Constructors' Cup was the title that interested him, as it was his cars that won races and his drivers who lost them. However, the drivers' title is the one that captures the imagination, and the record books show that the last Ferrari driver to win one was Jody Scheckter in 1979. Still, at least Ferrari came

PRAYING FOR SUCCESS: Ferrari's sporting boss Jean Todt kneels in prayer on the Ferrari pitwall

away from Suzuka last October with one title, having won the Constructors' Cup for the first time since 1983.

A glorious past

Look at Ferrari's history and it's easy to understand why it possesses such a mystique. Antonio Ascari, Juan Manuel Fangio, Mike Hawthorn, Phil Hill, John Surtees, Niki Lauda and Jody Scheckter have all won the world title as Ferrari drivers. But the last of these was in 1979, which is not what the *tifosi* – Ferrari fans – expect from a team with the largest budget of all. Indeed, in the mid-1990s, Ferrari was a team that appeared to have come off the rails. However, Jean Todt started to shape the team so that it could take the battle to the British teams. But progress was only made when Schumacher joined in 1996.

The German's skills have turned Ferrari from a team that won once in a blue moon to one that had a chance at every circuit. He won three times in 1996 in a chassis that would not have won in the hands of others. The following year, he won five times and went to the final round with a shot

CHECKING THE WEATHER: Ferrari's master tactician Ross Brawn looks to the sky for clues before the Japanese GP

FOR THE RECORD

Country of origin:	Italy
Team base:	Maranello, Italy
Date of formation:	1939
Active years in Formula One:	From 1950
Grands Prix contested:	619
Wins:	125
Pole positions:	127
Fastest laps:	139
Constructors' Cup victories:	1961, 1964, 1975, 1976, 1977, 1979, 1982, 1983, 1999

Drivers and Results 1999

Driver	Nationality	Races	Wins	Pts	Pos
Eddie Irvine	Northern Irish	16	4	74	2nd
Mika Salo	Finnish	6	0	10	10th
Michael Schumacher	German	10	2	44	5th

Car specifications

Sponsors:	Marlboro, Shell, TIM, Tic Tac
Team principal:	Jean Todt
Technical director:	Ross Brawn
Team manager:	Stefano Domienicali
Designer:	Rory Byrne
Chief engineer:	Giorgio Ascanelli
Test driver:	Luca Badoer
Chassis:	Ferrari F320
Engine:	Ferrari V10

at the title before losing out to Jacques Villeneuve at Jerez. He came close again in 1998 when he won six times and took Mika Hakkinen to the final round at Suzuka.

A fractured year

The thought of removing Schumacher from the equation for six of last year's Grands Prix and Ferrari still coming within an ace of taking both titles wouldn't have been countenanced even by people within Ferrari, such is the esteem with which he is held at Maranello. Yet, he broke his right leg on the opening lap of the British GP when his brakes failed at Stowe. He would miss six races and only return, rather grudgingly, for the season's final two races. And the reason that his smile was absent was that he returned in a supporting role to Irvine.

If Irvine enjoyed being Ferrari number one for the six races when Michael was convalescing and the two after he returned, he'd come away from the first race of the year in high spirits, too, as he picked up his first victory when the McLarens retired. However, it was Schumacher who was second at Interlagos then won the third and fourth races at Imola and Monaco. But Irvine was a frequent scorer and was in a position to challenge for honours when Schumacher suffered his accident at Silverstone. His position was strengthened further when he won in Austria and Germany, albeit helped by stand-in Mika Salo at Hockenheim.

Consistent driving rather than dominant form kept him in the hunt as Hakkinen's McLaren failed or lost out in inter-team battles, but when Schumacher returned for the Malaysian Grand Prix and helped Irvine to victory, he was set for the final round with a four-point lead. Headlines were made when both Ferraris were disqualified for a discrepancy on their bargeboards. But, a week later, they were reinstated by the court of appeal, leaving the FIA with egg on its face.

At the final round at Suzuka, Hakkinen got the jump on the pole-sitting Schumacher and motored off to victory, and there was nothing that Irvine could do about it, losing out in the title race by two points as he came home third.

MICHAEL SCHUMACHER

ONLY THE TITLE WILL DO

Michael Schumacher broke his leg and had his reputation sullied in 1999, so expect him to be out to prove that he's the world's best driver. Oh, and to try to become a champion for Ferrari.

HUNGRY FOR SUCCESS: Michael Schumacher didn't enjoy sitting on the sidelines in 1999 and is anxious to become champion for Ferrari

Last year didn't fit into Michael Schumacher's master-plan. For, not only did he break his right leg at the British Grand Prix, but his reputation was tarnished by Ferrari supremo Luca di Montezemolo saying that Michael appeared to be avoiding coming back to help Eddie Irvine gun for the title.

Michael said that he was in pain in the cockpit. Many said that there was no way he would want to help his erstwhile number two claim the target he himself is desperate to achieve, to become the first Ferrari driver to win the drivers' title since Jody Scheckter in 1979.

Whatever, Michael did return, helped Irvine to victory at Sepang and finished second behind Hakkinen at Suzuka. Whether he could have beaten the Finn is open to debate, as is whether he wanted to.

Michael was driving as well as ever last year and was only eight points behind Hakkinen before he broke his leg at Silverstone thanks to his wins at Imola and Monaco. Yet, crashing out of the lead at the Canadian Grand Prix showed that he was having to drive on the limit.

Looking to 2000, the world's best-paid driver has lost Irvine as his number two and has Rubens Barrichello, a driver who is not quite so sure that his role will be as number two. Indeed, di Montezemolo has said that he no longer wants the team to be so focused around one driver.

Backed to succeed

Michael was the hottest talent in German racing in the late 1980s. Guided into Formula Three by Willi Weber, he became champion in 1990 and beat Hakkinen at Macau. A works sportscar driver for Mercedes, Michael made his Formula One debut for Jordan at Spa in 1991. He moved immediately to Benetton for whom he regularly outqualified team-mate Nelson Piquet. His first win came at Spa a year later.

However, it all came right in 1994 and he won eight times. His title battle with Damon Hill came to a head in Adelaide when he clipped a wall and took both himself and Damon Hill out, and so became champion. Michael scored nine wins in 1995 to the four Hill managed in the superior Williams for his second title.

Joining Ferrari in 1996, Michael put the team back on track with three wins. That tally rose to five in 1997, but he had to give best to Williams's Jacques Villeneuve in a season that ended in a collision at Jerez. The 1998 season was Michael's best for Ferrari as he won six times to take the title battle to the final race. But he stalled on the grid at Suzuka and Hakkinen won the day.

TRACK NOTES

Nationality: . . . . .GERMAN
Born: . . . . .JANUARY 3, 1969,
. . . . .KERPEN, GERMANY
Teams: . . . . .JORDAN 1991,
. . . . .BENETTON 1991-1995,
. . . . .FERRARI 1996-2000

Career record

First Grand Prix: . . .1991 BELGIAN GP
Grand Prix starts: 128
Grand Prix wins: 35
*(1992 Belgian GP, 1993 Portuguese GP,
1994 Brazilian GP, 1994 Pacific GP,
1994 San Marino GP, 1994 Monaco GP,
1994 Canadian GP, 1994 French GP,
1994 Hungarian GP, 1994 European GP,
1995 Brazilian GP, 1995 Spanish GP,
1995 Monaco GP, 1995 French GP,
1995 German GP, 1995 Belgian GP,
1995 European GP, 1995 Pacific GP,
1995 Japanese GP, 1996 Spanish GP,
1996 Belgian GP, 1996 Italian GP,
1997 Monaco GP, 1997 Canadian GP,
1997 French GP, 1997 Belgian GP,
1997 Japanese GP, 1998 Argentinian GP,
1998 Canadian GP, 1998 French GP,
1998 British GP, 1998 Hungarian GP,
1998 Italian GP, 1999 San Marino GP,
1999 Monaco GP)*
Poles: .23
Fastest laps: 38
Points: 570
Honours: . . . .1995 & 1994 FORMULA
ONE WORLD CHAMPION, 1990
GERMAN FORMULA THREE CHAMPION
& MACAU GP WINNER, 1988 GERMAN
FORMULA KONIG CHAMPION

RUBENS BARRICHELLO

ALL CHANGE FOR 2000

Rubens Barrichello, Ferrari driver. That's the biggest change in the Brazilian's career and yet it's a gamble going to be number two to Michael Schumacher just as the team he has left, Jaguar Racing, is moving up a gear.

Rubens signed to join Ferrari around the time of last year's British Grand Prix, but it was months later that the deal was announced. And one matter was already sketchy. This was the small matter of his status within the team, with Rubens saying that he wouldn't be playing second fiddle to Michael Schumacher. This was later denied, but Ferrari supremo Luca di Montezemolo said last November that he no longer wanted the team to be focused on one driver. While this was great news for Rubens, many fear for the likeable but perhaps emotionally fragile Brazilian. After all, Schumacher hasn't achieved what he's achieved by helping his team-mates.

So, Rubens has taken a gamble, especially leaving behind the Stewart family who have nurtured him. However, the Ferrari should be the best car he's ever driven and Rubens will be desperate to land that first win that has eluded him through his 113 Grands Prix. And I can't think of a driver who will be more emotional when this happens.

finished just twice in 17 starts. Mind you, one of these finishes was second place at Monaco. Disappointingly, 1998 saw no progress, and with the exception of a pair of fifth places in Spain and Canada, Rubens seldom finished.

Looking for a more competitive ride, Rubens talked to Williams, but couldn't afford to buy his way out of his contract, so he stayed with Stewart and could easily have come away from the Australian Grand Prix with a win, judging by the pace he showed in the race. Trouble was, he started from the rear of the grid after a problem that triggered a re-start and then collected a stop-go penalty. Showing this was no fluke, he then sent the crowds wild by leading at Interlagos. Third place at Imola showed that he meant business, as did pole in the wet and then third place in the race at Magny-Cours. But Stewart appeared to go off the boil and only third place at the Nurburgring lifted the tail end of the season. And now his mind is on cars that are red...

A slow bloomer

Considering his natural speed, it's astonishing that Rubens hasn't yet won a Grand Prix. Rubens won the Formula Opel Euroseries in 1990 and the British Formula Three Championship in 1991, ahead of David Coulthard. After a mixed season in Formula 3000, he joined Jordan in 1993 and ran second to Ayrton Senna at Donington Park. But the next three years were fruitless except for second place in Canada in 1995. Then Jackie Stewart signed him to lead his new team. But 1997 yielded only six points in a year in which he

TRACK NOTES

Nationality: . . . . .BRAZILIAN
Born: . . . . MAY 23, 1972,
. . . . .SAO PAULO, BRAZIL
Teams: . . . . .JORDAN 1993-1996,
. . . . .STEWART 1997-1999,
. . . . .FERRARI 2000

Career record

First Grand Prix: 1993 SOUTH AFRICAN GP
Grand Prix starts: 113
Grand Prix wins: . . . . .NONE
*(best result: second, 1995
Canadian GP, 1997 Monaco GP)*
Poles: 2
Fastest laps: . . . . NONE
Points: .77
Honours: . . . .1991 BRITISH FORMULA
THREE CHAMPION, 1990 GM
EUROSERIES CHAMPION, 1988
BRAZILIAN KARTING CHAMPION

MAKE OR BREAK: This will be the greatest test of Rubens's career

JORDAN

ONWARDS AND UPWARDS

Jordan's aim last year was to move up a place to finish third overall in the Constructors' Cup. So, this year, the target must be second overall or even one higher.

USING THE THROTTLE: Team owner Eddie Jordan shows outgoing driver Damon Hill the most effective use of the throttle during a troubled final season for the Englishman

Eddie Jordan wanted to start a Formula One team. So he did so in 1991. Then he wanted his team to be taken seriously and that target was met too. The third step was to win a Grand Prix and that was achieved in 1998. Being thought of as one of the big three teams was the most recent step, something that was achieved last year. And that leaves winning the Constructors' Cup. However, this might take a few more years yet.

Eddie Jordan has high hopes for his team. Firstly, Heinz-Harald Frentzen is to be lead driver, anxious to add to the two wins he scored for the team last year when many considered him the driver of the year. Secondly, he is being joined by Jarno Trulli, a driver who some say has the most natural talent in Formula One today. This is his chance to prove it, especially as you can be sure that Mike Gascoyne will produce a

FOR THE RECORD

Country of origin: ....England
Team base: ....Silverstone, England
Date of formation: 1981
Active years in Formula One: ....From 1991
Grands Prix contested: 146
Wins: 3
Pole positions: 2
Fastest laps: 2

Drivers and Results 1999

Driver	Nationality	Races	Wins	Pts	Pos
Heinz-Harald Frentzen	German	16	2	54	3rd
Damon Hill	English	16	0	7	11th

Car specifications

Sponsors: ....Benson & Hedges, Deutsche Post
Team principal: ....Eddie Jordan
Technical director: ....Mike Gascoyne
Team manager: ....Trevor Foster
Chief engineer: ....Dino Toso
Test driver: ....tba
Chassis: ....Jordan EJ10
Engine: ....Mugen Honda V10

MAKING A NAME: Mike Gascoyne's star continues to be in the ascendancy as he enters his second full season with Jordan, running the technical side of the team

competitive chassis and Honda's engines are likely to be even better than in 1999 in the quest for helping the drivers onto a par with the McLarens and Ferraris. That said, the Jordan package is looking better than ever before and is likely to have both drivers scoring on a regular basis, something that it will need to do if it is to achieve Jordan's next target: second place in the Constructors' Cup.

A flying start

Jordan was a welcome addition when it moved up from Formula 3000 to Formula One in 1991 and it immediately looked like a team that belonged. Andrea de Cesaris even came close to giving the team its maiden victory when he chased Ayrton Senna's McLaren for the lead in the Belgian GP until his engine blew. They finished the year fifth overall. A works engine deal with Yamaha followed for 1992, but Stefano Modena and Mauricio Gugelmin scored just one point. There were no works engines for 1993. However, the paid-for Hart engines worked better and Rubens Barrichello shone in the European Grand Prix at Donington Park by running second behind Senna before retiring.

Jordan ranked fifth overall in 1994, but 1995 produced a day of days for Jordan in Canada when Barrichello and Eddie Irvine were second and third behind Alesi who'd raced for Jordan in Formula 3000. Sixth overall that year, they were fifth again in 1996 but neither Barrichello nor Martin Brundle recorded a top-three result.

Ralf Schumacher signed up for 1997 and stunned by finishing third in his third Grand Prix, albeit after nudging team-mate Giancarlo Fisichella out of the race... The points then started to flow from both drivers, with Fisichella even leading briefly at Hockenheim before suffering a puncture. He peaked with second place at Spa.

It all came right in 1998, albeit only after a first half of the year that offered the team nothing in the way of encouragement. Indeed, nowhere were the cars further off the pace than at Monaco where whey lined up on the eighth row. It wasn't until the ninth round that they finally scored their first point of the year, with Ralf rushing from the back of the field in the wet to finish sixth at Silverstone. The points then came in almost every Grand Prix and it all came together at Spa-Francorchamps where Damon Hill kept Ralf behind him for the team's first win and its only ever one-two to date. This and further good results led to Jordan wresting fourth place overall from Benetton at Suzuka.

A tale of two drivers

Armed with this victory, Hill was looking forward to his final season last year. He was being joined by Frentzen, with the press making a lot of the fact that the German was the driver who took his place at Williams in 1997, but the drivers never saw that as a reason not to get on. Trouble was, one of them got on rather better than the other, with Hill looking for the door by mid-season.

The reason for Hill's loss of desire was that he found the extra groove in the front tyres made the cars behave in a way he didn't like. Indeed, while Frentzen kicked off with a second place and then a third, Hill didn't score until the third round when he was fourth. He then had to wait until five rounds after that before he scored again, with a fifth. And apart from two more sixth places, that was that. Sadly, his heart wasn't always in it. The state of his relationship became clear after he parked up in the final race, as Eddie Jordan failed to mention him in the post-race press release.

Frentzen, on the other hand, was in fabulous form at every race, scoring a lottery of a win in the French GP and then a second win in the Italian Grand Prix as part of his tally that helped him rank third overall.

HEINZ-HARALD FRENTZEN

MAN WITH THE GOLDEN CAR

Heinz-Harald Frentzen's reputation was gilded last year when he bounced back from rejection at Williams to shine for Jordan. Expect him to blossom yet more in the year ahead.

Heinz-Harald Frentzen was the revelation of 1999. It's not that anyone ever doubted the German's natural speed. It's just that it had been submerged at Williams. But his former Formula 3000 boss Eddie Jordan offered Heinz-Harald a chance to blossom and he attacked from the outset with Jordan's excellent Mugen Honda-powered chassis.

Second place at the season-opener in Melbourne owed a lot to the retirement of both McLarens and Michael Schumacher starting from the back, but he'd laid down a marker by qualifying four places ahead of team-mate Damon Hill – the driver he replaced at Williams. But Damon failed to respond as he struggled with the car and Heinz-Harald made hay, finishing third on his second time out at Interlagos. Fourth place followed at Monaco. But his season really took off when Heinz-Harald used a bold fuel strategy in the French GP and scored Jordan's second win.

A run of five races in which he finished either third or fourth followed and suddenly people realised that Heinz-Harald was making up ground as Mika Hakkinen continued to drop points. Indeed, when the Finn spun out of the lead at Monza, who was there to pick up the win but Heinz-Harald. Now in the thick of the championship chase, it all seemed to be coming his way when he led at the Nurburgring, but his car failed and he came away with nothing. Unable to win either of the final two Grands Prix, Heinz-Harald slipped to third overall, but it had been a stunning season, and one in which

he scored 54 points to Hill's seven.

The big question is whether Heinz-Harald will be able to improve on this in the season ahead. If Hakkinen and McLaren get their act together and Michael Schumacher doesn't take a six-race sabbatical, the answer is probably that third place overall will be all he can expect. But if Honda can provide a boost in horsepower, then you never know...

Formula One via Japan

Heinz-Harald was German Formula Opel champion in 1988. Runner-up in German Formula Three in 1989, he joined Mercedes' sportscar squad, but concentrated on Formula 3000. No success followed, so he moved to Japanese Formula 3000 in 1992 before graduating to Formula One with Sauber in 1994. After peaking with third place at Monza in 1995, he found his position in the team usurped by Johnny Herbert in 1996 and left for Williams in 1997. Heinz-Harald won at Imola, but this was his only one while team-mate Jacques Villeneuve won six. There was an improvement

in his relationship with the team in 1998, but still the results didn't come, with third in Australia his best result.

TRACK NOTES

Nationality: . . . . .GERMAN
Born: . . . . .MAY 18, 1967,
.MOENCHENGLADBACH, GERMANY
Teams: . . . . . . .SAUBER 1994–1996,
. . . . .WILLIAMS 1997–98,
. . . . .JORDAN 1999–2000

Career record
First Grand Prix: .1994 BRAZILIAN GP
Grand Prix starts: 97
Grand Prix wins: 3
(1997 San Marino GP,
1999 French GP, 1999 Italian GP)
Poles: 2
Fastest laps: 6
Points: 143
Honours: . . .1989 GERMAN FORMULA
THREE RUNNER-UP, 1988 GERMAN
FORMULA OPEL CHAMPION, 1984
GERMAN JUNIOR KARTING CHAMPION

A MAN REINVENTED: Heinz-Harald Frentzen arrived at Jordan with his tail between his legs. But then...

JARNO TRULLI

WATCH HIM FLY

Jarno Trulli was hailed as the next great thing when he arrived in Formula One back in 1997. It then went quiet. But now that he's joined Jordan, expect to see him fly — he could even win a race or two. So, watch out!

Nationality: . . . . .ITALIAN
Born: . . . . .JULY 13, 1974,
. . . . .PESCARA, ITALY
Teams: . . . . .MINARDI 1997,
. . . . .PROST 1997–1999,
. . . . .JORDAN 2000

Career record

First Grand Prix: 1997 AUSTRALIAN GP
Grand Prix starts: 46
Grand Prix wins: . . . . .NONE
(best result: second,
1999 European GP)
Poles: . . . . .NONE
Fastest laps: . . . . .NONE
Points: 11
Honours: . . . . .1996 GERMAN
FORMULA THREE CHAMPION,
1994 WORLD KARTING CHAMPION

THE FUTURE LOOKS BRIGHT: Jarno Trulli started to set competitive times the second he started testing for Jordan at the end of 1999. He should keep Frentzen on his toes

Up until last year's European Grand Prix at the Nurburgring, Jarno Trulli had scored just one point in the year's first 13 Grands Prix. This was for a hard-fought sixth place at the Spanish Grand Prix. So people said maybe he wasn't as brilliant as he'd once been considered. However, they'd ignored the fact that the Peugeot-powered Prost was perhaps not the car to have in 1999. And it wasn't just Jarno who was struggling, as team-mate Olivier Panis only had two sixth places to his name.

But then Jarno drove a superb race in the changing weather conditions in the European Grand Prix at the Nurburgring to finish second, fighting mightily to resist Rubens Barrichello's faster Stewart in the closing laps. While this drive must have thrilled Alain Prost as it moved his team up one position in the Constructors' Cup, it must have thrilled Eddie Jordan even more, for he was the one who had Jarno's name

on a contract for the season ahead.

With the Jordan-Mugen Honda combination expected to be even more competitive in 2000, Jarno will have a regular chance to go for points and even for podium finishes. And, as shown by his new team-mate Heinz-Harald Frentzen, wins could even be in the offing.

Straight to the top

Jarno was the star of world karting when he was spotted by former Benetton boss Flavio Briatore and propelled direct to Formula Three midway through 1995, running in the German championship. He won the final two races and returned in 1996 to win the title. Confident in the manner of the late Ayrton Senna, Jarno said that Formula 3000 would be an unnecessary extra step for him...

So it was that he made it to Formula One the following year, after less than two years in car

racing, when a last-minute deal took Jarno to Minardi in 1997. Despite next to no pre-season testing, Jarno did all that could be expected of him, gaining valuable race mileage. But then he was propelled onto a higher plane when Olivier Panis broke his legs and he stood in for him at Prost. Jarno scored his first points, with fourth place at Hockenheim, then qualified third at the A1-Ring, got the jump on Michael Schumacher and took the lead when Mika Hakkinen retired on the first lap. Jarno led until his pitstop. Jacques Villeneuve moved ahead and Jarno was running second ahead of David Coulthard when his engine blew.

With Prost full-time in 1998, Jarno had a disappointing time. He generally outqualified Panis and scored the team's only point with sixth place in the battle-torn Belgian Grand Prix, but the majority of last year's races ended with mechanical failure.

WILLIAMS

TIME TO BOUNCE BACK

Armed with new works engines from BMW, Williams will be looking to rediscover its glorious winning ways of old after two seasons in the wilderness with only Ralf Schumacher's form saving last year.

THE VIPs

Frank Williams

A successful driver up to Formula Three, Frank took up team ownership in 1969, running a Formula One Brabham for Piers Courage. Was dealt a bodyblow when Courage died in 1970, but kept going on his own and got his big break in late 1970s when he landed Saudi-backing and the team soon hit winning form. He has been confined to a wheelchair since a road accident in 1988.

Patrick Head

Patrick went straight to Lola after graduating in mechanical engineering and had his first crack at Formula One in 1976 with the Wolf-Williams team. The team split and he started a partnership with Frank Williams that has produced 103 Grand Prix wins so far. Patrick is now more involved with operations than design.

STILL SMILING: Frank Williams has been around long enough to know that Formula One can be cyclical and he's looking forward to 2000

It's amazing how fast matters change in Formula One. Last year people were lauding Ralf Schumacher's efforts to drag his Williams into the points and occasionally to a placing good enough for him to join in the podium ceremony and yet, as recently as 1997, a Williams number one would have been disappointed to have finished second. Yet, this team which was Constructors' Cup champion in 1992, 1993, 1994, 1996 and 1997 slipped to fifth in the rankings, overtaken by Jordan and Stewart.

It would be easy to blame their woes on the fact that there was no works engine deal and they had to struggle with Supertec engines that were reputed to give away 60bhp to the works engines enjoyed by all the teams ahead of them. However, the FW21 chassis didn't appear to be the equal of the standard-setting McLaren MP4-14. And, while Schumacher performed what were seen as near miracles in making up for these shortcomings, his team-mate did not. No, two-time Indycar champion Alessandro Zanardi's return to Formula One was not the success that everyone had hoped it would be. Indeed, he retired more often than not and was only in touch with Ralf at the Italian Grand Prix after a late-season boost in form. An intelligent driver, he struggled to work out how to drive a car that was not only vastly different to the Indycar he'd vacated, but also to the Formula One cars of old. Yet, consider the problems that Damon Hill had all year and Johnny Herbert suffered in the first half of the year, and it was clear that these precise and smooth drivers were at a disadvantage with the four-groove rubber. However, prompted by the desires of BMW, the team terminated Zanardi's contract and replaced him with Jorg Muller to create an all-German team.

Enter BMW . . .

So, although the driver line up has changed for 2000, the design team is remaining constant. So, the only notable change is on the engine front. And notable it is, as Williams will be running works engines for the first time since 1997, its most recent championship-winning year. They will not

FOR THE RECORD

Country of origin: . . . . .England
Team base: . . . . .Grove, England
Date of formation: 1968
Active years in Formula One: . . . . .From 1973
Grands Prix contested: 411
Wins: 103
Pole positions: 108
Fastest laps: 111
Constructors' Cup victories: 1980, 1981, 1986,
. . . . .1987, 1992, 1993, 1994, 1996, 1997

Drivers and Results 1999

Driver	Nationality	Races	Wins	Pts	Pos
Ralf Schumacher	German	16	0	35	6th
Alessandro Zanardi	Italian	15	0	0	N/A

Car specifications

Sponsors: . . . . .BMW
Team principal: . . . . .Frank Williams
Technical director: . . . . .Patrick Head
Team manager: . . . . .Dickie Stanford
Chief engineer: . . . . .James Robinson
Test driver: . . . . .Bruno Junqueira
Chassis: . . . . .Williams FW22
Engine: . . . . .BMW V10

be from Renault this time, though, but from BMW, the German marque making its return to Formula One since it left in 1987, when it provided engines for Brabham.

The engine tested extensively last year in a year-old Williams chassis, with Jorg Muller doing the early mileage. It was hard to gauge progress, with rumours circulating that not only was it down on horsepower, but that it was also too heavy. BMW Motorsport boss Gerhard Berger had to deny stories last October that the plug was to be pulled. So, perhaps this will be another interim season for Williams and its drivers after all. Still, at least Ralf was rewarded with a hefty wage rise, much of which comes from BMW which is taking over the sponsorship of the team following the withdrawal of Winfield.

Honing a talent

At the start of last year, there was a very different feel to Williams as both drivers were new to the team, with Alessandro arriving with the 1997 and 1998 Indycar titles under his belt, while Ralf joined from Jordan in a straight swap with Heinz-Harald Frentzen. Many felt that Ralf would find it as hard to get on with the Williams management, and Head in particular, as Frentzen had. But how wrong they were, as their relationship worked from the very beginning, as third place in the Australian GP – one place behind Frentzen – showed. This was no flash in the pan, as Ralf had clearly matured after two seasons in which noone doubted his speed but many feared for his safety. It was Zanardi who struggled. If there was bad luck going, it seemed to go his way, but he was dominated by Ralf in qualifying as well as the races, so all was clearly not right.

Ralf proved himself by far the best of the six drivers using Supertec engines and along with a cluster of fourth places, also visited the podium at Silverstone and Monza. And, had it not been for a puncture in the European Grand Prix at the Nurburgring, he could well have given Williams its first victory since Jacques Villeneuve won the Luxembourg Grand Prix at the same circuit at the end ot his championship year.

SWAPPING STORIES: Williams's Patrick Head catches up on the pitlane gossip with Ferrari's Ross Brawn. And you can rest assured that he won't be wanting to see the red Italian cars leave his cars behind again this year

RALF SCHUMACHER

NOW ONE OF THE STARS

Ralf Schumacher was a changed man last year, showing remarkable maturity alongside his undoubted speed. Now he has just got to hope that the BMW engines are good enough to help him score his first Grand Prix victory.

GOOD NEWS ONLY, PLEASE: Ralf Schumacher blocks out news of how fast the McLarens and Ferraris have gone. His focus is on success

dependent on the form of the new works BMW engines that Williams will be using this year.

That said, the weakest point of the Williams package last year was the Supertec engines it used, with Ralf giving away an appreciable amount of horsepower to his rivals. But he started the year with third place at Melbourne and kept it going from there, making next to no mistakes and scoring more often than not as team-mate Alessandro Zanardi failed to score even once. No wonder Williams technical chief Patrick Head appreciated Ralf's efforts.

Second place with fastest lap at the Italian Grand Prix was the highlight of Ralf's year, but the real highlight should have been the European Grand Prix at the Nurburgring where a blow-out robbed Ralf of what would have been his maiden win. All in all, he deserved a better final ranking than sixth overall.

Looking to 2000, expect him to remain unchallenged as the team's top dog, with his team-mate unlikely to trouble him.

A fast riser

Like his elder brother Michael, Ralf spent his childhood at their father's karting circuit. Ralf then went directly to Formula Three in 1994, driving for the team owned by Willi Weber, Michael's manager. He scored his first win at the end of the season to end up third overall then had a straight fight with Norberto Fontana in 1995, with the Argentinian taking the

TRACK NOTES

Nationality: . . . . .GERMAN
Born: . . . . .30 JUNE 1975,
. . . . .KERPEN, GERMANY
Teams: . . . . . .JORDAN 1997–1998,
. . . . .WILLIAMS 1999–2000

Career record

First Grand Prix: 1997 AUSTRALIAN GP
Grand Prix starts: 49
Grand Prix wins: . . . . .NONE
(best result: second, 1998 Belgian GP & 1999 Italian GP)
Poles: . . . . .NONE
Fastest laps: 1
Points: 62
Honours: . . . . .1996 FORMULA NIPPON CHAMPION, 1995 GERMAN FORMULA THREE RUNNER-UP & WON 1995 MACAU FORMULA THREE GP

honours. They met again in Formula Nippon in 1996, and Ralf landed the title in the final round.

When Ralf arrived in Formula One with Jordan in 1997, people dismissed him as simply being Michael's brother. But they had to reassess their views in the third race when he finished third in the Argentinian Grand Prix. However, he was largely outraced and outpsyched by team-mate Giancarlo Fisichella. And he crashed too often. Ralf cleaned up his act in 1998 after some wild moments in the early races. Indeed, not only did Ralf collect Jordan's first points of the year at Silverstone, but he did so from the back of the grid. Then the points started to flow, although he didn't enjoy being told to stay behind Damon in the closing laps of the Belgian Grand Prix when the team didn't want to risk jeopardizing its first victory.

Ralf swapped seats with Heinz-Harald Frentzen for last year, moving from Jordan to Williams, and both compatriots shone as never before. Many rated them as the drivers of the year as they took the battle to the drivers of the superior McLarens and Ferraris. Now, what Ralf must do is to keep this momentum going in 2000. But he is largely

JORG MULLER

PERSEVERANCE REWARDED

Being a test driver for BMW paid off for Jorg Muller as he landed the second Williams seat after Alessandro Zanardi's enforced departure.

TRACK NOTES

Nationality: . . . . .GERMAN
Born: . . . . .SEPTEMBER 3, 1969,
. . . . .KERKRADE, HOLLAND
Teams: . . . . .WILLIAMS 2000

Career record

First Grand Prix: 2000 AUSTRALIAN GP
Grand Prix starts: . . . . .NONE
Grand Prix wins: . . . . .NONE
Poles: . . . . .NONE
Fastest laps: . . . . .NONE
Points: . . . . .NONE
Honours: . .1999 SEBRING 12 HOURS,
1996 FORMULA 3000 CHAMPION,
1994 GERMAN F3 CHAMPION,
1993 MACAU F3 GP,
1991 MONACO F3 GP,
1989 GERMAN FORMULA OPEL
LOTUS CHAMPION

Jorg Muller is a driver who has long been worthy of a Formula One break. But he appeared to have been afflicted by a curse that has befallen almost every one of the Formula 3000 champions since the category was created from Formula Two in 1985. That is to say, no Formula One career to speak of, while the hot seats have gone to the lesser lights.

Formula 3000 champion in 1996, Jorg has been in the wilderness ever since. Sure, he was Sauber's test driver in 1998 and BMW test driver in 1999, but that hardly kept him busy, especially last year as he waited for the BMW to be ready. And, all this time, very successful forays for BMW in sportscars aside, he had to watch younger compatriot Nick Heidfeld shine in Formula 3000 and then waltz straight into a drive with Prost for 2000.

However, before 1999 was out, Jorg was finally told the news that he had been waiting at least a month to hear. Namely, Alessandro Zanardi had been told by Williams – at engine supplier BMW's behest – that his services weren't required for the second year of his contract. And, with this happening long after the top seats were filled, there were no top drivers available to replace him. So, enter BMW's Jorg, with a dream drive handed to him on a plate.

Looking at the task ahead, Jorg is obviously hoping that the new BMW engine will prove competitive in its first season and that the Williams design team comes up with a chassis that won't be inferior to those from Ferrari and McLaren. However, Jorg also has to hope that he will not be left behind by team-mate Ralf Schumacher, a driver the team really took to its heart last year.

A collector of titles

After trying Formula Ford in 1988, Jorg won the German Formula Opel Lotus series in 1989. Jorg showed well in Formula Three in 1990 as Michael Schumacher cleaned up and Jorg ended up fifth. But, while Schumacher became a Formula One driver in 1991, it would take Jorg rather longer... Indeed, he wasn't clear of the formula until the end of 1994 when he became German champion, having also won the street races at Monaco and Macau on the way.

Without the money to race in Formula 3000 in 1995, Jorg raced for BMW in German Super Touring, starting a relationship that has just borne fruit in the biggest way possible.

Jorg made it to Formula 3000 in 1996 and proceeded to win the crown after a season-long battle with Kenny Brack. But a Formula One race seat failed to beckon and Jorg entered into his diet of the odd Formula One test session and sportscars.

**A MOVE INTO THE BIG TIME:
Opportunity knocks for Jorg as he
steps into Zanardi's shoes for 2000**

JAGUAR RACING

NEW NAME, NEW COLOURS

After three years, Stewart Grand Prix is no more. From this year on, Ford's buyout of the team means that it will race as Jaguar Racing, a great name from sportscar racing looking to make its mark in Formula One.

THE VIPs

Jackie Stewart

One of Britain's best ever drivers, as three Formula One world titles attest, Jackie kept involved through commentary work and forming a team to guide son Paul through the junior categories. Then he took the plunge with Paul in 1997 and entered his own team in Formula One. This was sold to Ford to run as Jaguar Racing in 2000, with Jackie staying on at the helm.

Gary Anderson

Gary joined Brabham in 1972, then moved on to McLaren five years later as chief mechanic. The Ulsterman left in 1980 and formed Anson, building Formula Three chassis. After a spell in Indycars from 1985 to 1987, Gary helped Roberto Moreno to the Formula 3000 title before being a founder member of Jordan, working as chief designer until he moved to Stewart at the end of 1998.

The Ford Motor Company is perhaps the most motorsport-minded of the major motor manufacturers, as its record number of 150 plus Formula One victories will attest. But that was largely thanks to the inspired sponsorship of Cosworth's DFV engine in the 1960s, a deal that kept the Ford name up in lights in Formula One until the early 1980s. Since then, though, Ford has slipped, taken its eye off the ball and made recent forays into Formula One less successfully than they would have liked. But now it's time to get serious and Ford's head honcho Jac Nasser has got involved. As a consequence, instead of employing teams such as Stewart to shape Ford's fortune in

A REDUCED ROLE: The arrival of Ford means that Paul Stewart won't have such a big role in Jaguar Racing

FOR THE RECORD

Country of origin: . . . . .England
Team base: .Milton Keynes, England
Date of formation: . . . . .1987 as Paul Stewart Racing
Active years in Formula One: . . . . .From 1997 (as Stewart)
Grands Prix contested: 49
Wins: 1
Pole positions: 1
Fastest laps: . . . . .None

Drivers and Results 1999

Driver	Nationality	Races	Wins	Pts	Pos
Rubens Barrichello	Brazilian	16	0	21	7th
Johnny Herbert	English	16	1	15	8th

Car specifications

Sponsors: . . . . .Jaguar, HSBC, MCI Worldcom, Hewlett Packard
Team principal: . . . . .Jackie Stewart
Team manager: . . . . .Dave Stubbs
Designers: . . . . .Gary Anderson & John Russell
Chief engineer: . . . . .Andy Miller
Test driver: . . . . .Luciano Burti
Chassis: . . . . .Jaguar R1
Engine: . . . . .Ford V10

Formula One, it has bought the team and will henceforth take control of its own destiny. This means that anything less than outright success will be considered a failure. However, everyone in the paddock was delighted to see Stewart land a maiden win that it had looked as though it would be denied by the Ford takeover, with Johnny Herbert delivering the goods at last autumn's European Grand Prix at the Nurburgring.

So, exit Stewart Grand Prix and enter Jaguar Racing, with new signing Eddie Irvine champing at the bit to resume the winning ways he so got to enjoy with Ferrari last season.

The cars will be painted in British Racing Green in a bid to make the most of Jaguar's fabulous sporting heritage. But this is how it should be with two British drivers in Irvine and Herbert. Ford's marketing arm will be working tirelessly to promote its Jaguar sportscar and sports saloon brand, one that has hitherto been associated with sportscar racing and the Le Mans 24 Hours in which it has been so successful.

With one of the best V10 engines in the business and a chassis from the pen of the vastly respected Gary Anderson, the package will be a good one. And with two top-rate drivers in Irvine and Herbert, a stream of good results should follow. Whether they will be able to topple McLaren and Ferrari from the top of the tree remains perhaps for a future season, but

FORD'S FIGUREHEAD: Jackie Stewart remains a hugely important factor in the outfit, even now that Ford's money means that the team is known as Jaguar Racing

the big-hitters at Ford's Detroit headquarters will consider anything less than third in the Constructors' Cup a failure.

How it all began

The roots of Jaguar Racing, born as Stewart Grand Prix, lie in Paul Stewart Racing, a team formed in 1987 when Paul decided to try racing. The team grew with Jackie's input and built a 'staircase of talent', entering cars in Formula Opel, Formula Three and Formula 3000. In other words, all the way from club racing to one step beneath Formula One. And it ran some great drivers, such as David Coulthard. However, it was still a huge jump when Stewart Grand Prix was formed and leapt into Formula One in 1997. There was much promise with drivers Rubens Barrichello and Jan Magnussen showing that the Ford engine had horsepower aplenty. However, it was also fragile and there were far too many retirements, although Barrichello did well by finishing second in Monaco.

The second year proved harder, and the mechanical failures continued, frustrating both Barrichello and Magnussen, and later Magnussen's replacement Jos Verstappen. However, the Dutchman failed to do any better than the Dane, and Barrichello ended the year as the team's top scorer with only four points.

Third time lucky

In their final season, Stewart went rather better, although it didn't look that way at the first race when both cars caught fire on the grid... However, Barrichello flew from the back of the grid in Melbourne and could have won the race but for a stop–go penalty. He then led the Brazilian Grand Prix before finishing third at Imola. A further third place followed at the French Grand Prix after he'd chosen the driest moment in a wet session to qualify on pole. However, this was nothing next to the team's day-of-days at the Nurburgring when wet weather was again part of the equation. Again Barrichello finished third. But what really made the Stewart team leap with delight was that this was two places behind the frequently unlucky Herbert who had read the changing conditions better than anyone else and given the team the win it so craved before the handover to Ford, helping the team to finish fourth in the Constructors' Cup.

EDDIE IRVINE

A NEW CHALLENGE

Eddie Irvine took last year's title battle to the final round and may never get as close again, but he will be relishing finally becoming a number one, albeit with Jaguar Racing, a team not yet as lofty as Ferrari.

Eddie Irvine hoped last year that he would win a Grand Prix – and he did that in the opening race. But he can never have expected to be Ferrari's number one driver for half of the season. And he certainly can't have expected to have reached the final round with a four point lead. Trouble was, the dream ended there as he came away from Suzuka as runner-up to Mika Hakkinen.

Last year was Eddie's fourth as number two to Michael Schumacher at Ferrari, so there was no reason to expect that he would be able to win unless the McLarens hit trouble and Michael was out of the reckoning, as that's what his contract stipulated. However, this is what happened in Melbourne. Ever the realist, though, Eddie pointed out that Ferrari couldn't rely on McLaren retirements.

And how right he was. But Eddie kept scoring points. Indeed, save for retiring from third place at Imola, he finished every race and he was outside the points only when he finished seventh in the European Grand Prix. But the turning point came at Silverstone when Schumacher broke his leg. Eddie went on to finish second. Victory in Austria and Germany showed that Ferrari could win without Schumacher. However, he'd received an assist in both, as he did when he won in Malaysia, and the reality was that Eddie was kept in the chase by McLaren's mistakes. That's not to say that Eddie didn't drive well, but the gap in speed to Hakkinen was shown at Suzuka when he was roundly beaten. And even if Schumacher

THE WORLD EXPECTS: Eddie Irvine will face not only racing for a new team, but also raised expectations

had let him through to second place, to finish equal on points with Hakkinen, Eddie would have lost out with four wins to the Finn's five.

From red to green

Eddie made his name by winning the British Formula Ford title and Festival in 1987. He ranked fifth in the British Formula Three series in 1989, a year dominated by JJ Lehto, and graduated to Formula 3000 in 1989. Despite finishing third overall for Eddie Jordan Racing in 1990, he received no offers of a Formula One ride and moved to Japanese Formula 3000, finishing as runner-up in 1993.

Eddie's Formula One break came at the end of 1993 when he was offered a ride in the Japanese Grand Prix by Jordan, scoring a point first time out. Staying with Jordan for 1994 and 1995, Eddie peaked with third at Montreal in 1995. He equalled that on his first race for Ferrari in 1996, but spent that season, 1997 and 1998 very much as number two to Michael Schumacher. But, having been given a taste of being a number one, he could take no more at Ferrari and this is why he signed for Jaguar.

TRACK NOTES

Nationality: . . . . . .NORTHERN IRISH
Born: . . . . .NOVEMBER 10, 1965,
. . . .CONLIG, NORTHERN IRELAND
Teams: . . . . . . .JORDAN 1993–1995,
. . . . .FERRARI 1996–1999,
. . . . .JAGUAR RACING 2000

Career record
First Grand Prix: . .1993 JAPANESE GP
Starts: 97
Wins: 4
(1999 Australian GP, 1999 Austrian GP, 1999 German GP, 1999 Malaysian GP)
Pole positions: . . . . .NONE
Fastest laps: 1
Points: 173
Honours: . .1993 JAPANESE FORMULA 3000 RUNNER-UP, 1987 BRITISH FORMULA FORD CHAMPION & FORMULA FORD FESTIVAL WINNER

JOHNNY HERBERT

NOT FINISHED YET

TRACK NOTES

Nationality: . . . . .ENGLISH
Born: . . . . .JUNE 27, 1964,
. . . . .ROMFORD, ENGLAND
Teams: .BENETTON & TYRRELL 1989,
. . . . .LOTUS 1991–1994,
. . . . .LIGIER 1994,
. . . . .BENETTON 1994–1995,
. . . . .SAUBER 1996–1998,
STEWART/JAGUAR RACING 1999/2000

Career record

First Grand Prix: .1989 BRAZILIAN GP
Grand Prix starts: 145
Grand Prix wins: 3
(1995 British GP, 1995 Italian GP,
1999 European GP)
Poles: . . . . .NONE
Fastest laps: . . . . .NONE
Points: 98
Honours: . .1991 LE MANS 24 HOURS
WINNER, 1987 BRITISH FORMULA
THREE CHAMPION, 1985 FORMULA
FORD FESTIVAL WINNER

Johnny Herbert was seen by some in 1999 as yesterday's man but he won the European Grand Prix for Stewart and his form improved from there. So, don't expect Eddie Irvine to have things all his own way at Jaguar.

Johnny Herbert is famous for his ready smile. He's also famous for his rotten luck. If there is a mechanical failure to be had, it usually happens to whatever car Johnny is driving. On top of this, people started to say that he was too old. Yet with his departure already planned by many of the sport's insiders, Johnny slotted it to his critics by winning the European Grand Prix.

So, Johnny kept his seat with Jaguar Racing, as it's now called, and will keep team leader Eddie Irvine on his toes. It will be an intriguing contest that won't be as one-sided as last year's runner-up will have you believe.

However, for much of 1999, Johnny was out of sorts, outperformed by his team-mate Rubens Barrichello. He said that he struggled to get the most out of his car, much like Damon Hill at Jordan. But a new differential was fitted at the Austrian Grand Prix and it started to come together. His victory came when he read the conditions best at the Nurburgring, but he showed that this was no fluke by finishing fourth in the next race at Sepang, only falling behind Mika Hakkinen near the end. By season's end, it was he not Barrichello who was top dog at Stewart, with the team more than happy to honour the second year of his contract.

Heading for the top

Johnny won the 1985 Formula Ford Festival. Despite having no backing, Eddie Jordan snapped him up for 1987 and he rewarded him with the British Formula Three title. Johnny won first time out in Formula 3000, but his year was curtailed by a foot-shattering accident at Brands Hatch on the day he'd signed to drive for Benetton for 1989. After a winter of physiotherapy, Johnny stunned by finishing fourth first time out, just ten seconds behind winner Nigel Mansell. He was the hottest talent to hit Formula One for years. But it became clear that his injuries weren't healed and he was cast into the wilderness. Johnny rebuilt his career in Japanese Formula 3000, then Lotus signed him for 1991. Trouble was, the team was in decline through to his departure at the end of 1994.

Life at Benetton in 1995 saw him challenge team-mate Michael Schumacher at the first race, but then the team concentrated on the German. However, Johnny won the British and Italian Grands Prix before heading to Sauber for 1996. By 1997, he was team leader and his third place in Hungary equalled Sauber's then best ever result. Sixth place in the 1998 season-opener at Melbourne looked promising but these were Johnny's only points and he soon found himself demoted to the team's number two seat by Jean Alesi and was only too delighted to join Stewart.

A CHALLENGE AHEAD: Johnny Herbert doesn't see himself as number two. So expect him to keep Eddie Irvine on his toes in 2000

BENETTON

STRUGGLING FOR GRIP

Last year, it was hard to imagine that this was the team that won the Constructors' Cup in 1995. And, without a works engine deal, don't expect fireworks from Benetton this year.

Benetton had a dreadful season last year. Upset to have fallen to fifth overall at the final round in 1998, they will have been drained by dropping another rung to sixth in the Constructors' Cup in 1999. And David Richards, the team boss who was shown the door before the end of the 1998 season, has every reason to smirk and say 'I told you so' to Rocco Benetton, the member of the team-owning family who replaced him.

It seems that the team's problems were threefold. Firstly, there was the fact that their Playlife-badged Supertec engines were no match for the works engines enjoyed by McLaren, Ferrari, Jordan and Stewart. Secondly, the chassis proved a nightmare as it failed to perform on circuits with high-speed corners, with the team taking the radical step mid-season of literally going back to the drawing board. Sadly, even this didn't work. As for its Front Torque Transfer system, that sank without trace. The third problem was probably related to this in that many said the team's drivers, Giancarlo Fisichella and Alexander Wurz, didn't have the technical experience to find a decent set-up. Yes, they had raced strongly in 1998, but insiders say that this was probably as a result of

HEIGHT OF FASHION: As expected from a team owned by a clothing manufacturer, Benetton's pitwear is among the most fashionable

FOR THE RECORD

Country of origin:	England
Team base:	Enstone, England
Date of formation:	1986
Active years in Formula One:	From 1986
Grands Prix contested:	327
Pole positions:	16
Fastest laps:	35
Constructors' Cup victories:	1995

Drivers and Results 1999

Driver	Nationality	Races	Wins	Pts	Pos
Giancarlo Fisichella	Italian	16	0	13	9th
Alexander Wurz	Austrian	16	0	3	13th

Car specifications

Sponsors:	Playlife, Mild Seven
Team principal:	Rocco Benetton
Team manager:	Joan Villadelprat
Designers:	Ben Agathangelou, Tim Densham & Chris Radage
Chief engineer:	Pat Symonds
Test driver:	tba
Chassis:	Benetton B200
Engine:	Playlife V10

A BRAVE SMILE: Benetton boss Rocco Benetton put on a brave face as the team struggled in 1999, but it will be harder to do this year if the team's form fails to improve

the chassis input from the team's experienced drivers from the 1997 season, Jean Alesi and Gerhard Berger.

Fisichella, on points

Looking at their race form through last season, Fisichella came out ahead, not only on points but also on consistent performance. After all, he claimed the team's 1999 high-spot of second in the Canadian Grand Prix, and was heading for a shock victory in the surprising European Grand Prix before he mimicked David Coulthard and threw his car off the track and into retirement. Wurz, who was fourth five times in 1998, never finished higher than fifth last season. On top of this, Fisichella almost invariably outqualified him. However, Benetton scarcely picked up a point in the second half of the year, echoing their tailing off in 1998, which perhaps is indicative of their failure to develop their chassis much from its starting point.

So, what is going to change for the 2000 season? On paper, not a lot, with Benetton again battling with a Playlife engine. Mind you, Supertec has promised more horsepower for this year. But, then again, every other engine builder will be looking to do the same, so this is no guarantee of success. So Benetton's courting of Renault in the hope of landing its works engine on the French giant's return in 2001 must be a priority.

On the chassis front, Nick Wirth has departed with a trio of up-and-coming designers in Ben Agathangelou, Tim Densham and Chris Radage

having been drafted into the line-up in the hope of finding a design that will go some way to closing the gap with McLaren, Jordan and Stewart on the chassis front.

The drivers will remain as before, marking the third year of their partnership, with Wurz in particular desperate to re-establish his reputation after it took a battering in 1999.

Whether this combination can gel and return to previous form remains to be seen. But, all things considered, it doesn't look as though Benetton's drivers will be challenging for race wins. A place on the podium would be seen as a triumph.

A fading past

To understand Benetton's history, one should not look back to the team's beginning when it took over the Toleman team for the start of the 1986 season, but rather look at what it did in the 1990s. Its masterstroke was to snatch Michael Schumacher away from Jordan at the end of 1991. For it was the German rather than Nelson Piquet, Benetton's previous number one, who put the team on the right track. The wins started as a trickle in 1992 before turning into a flood that saw him win the drivers' title in 1994 and 1995, with Benetton earning its one Constructors' Cup in 1995. But then Schumacher left for Ferrari and it took until the second half of 1997 for Berger to give Benetton its only win since. The supply of works Ford and then Renault engines dried up at the end of 1997, and the rest you know.

GIANCARLO FISICHELLA

A CAREER NEEDING A BOOST

Giancarlo Fisichella is in danger of not being seen as a bright young thing. And, unless Benetton makes progress this year, his star will be on the wane, his natural speed wasted. So, all in all, it's a crunch year for the Roman.

HIGHLY FAVOURED: Giancarlo Fisichella was kept smiling by his second place in Canada in 1999, but by little else in a troubled year

TRACK NOTES

Nationality: . . . . .ITALIAN
Born: . . . . .JANUARY 14, 1973,
. . . . .ROME, ITALY
Teams: . . . . .MINARDI 1996,
. . . . .JORDAN 1997,
. . . . .BENETTON 1998–2000

Career record
First Grand Prix: 1996 AUSTRALIAN GP
Grand Prix starts: 57
Grand Prix wins: . . . . .NONE
(best result: second, 1997 Belgian GP, 1998 Monaco GP, 1998 Canadian GP, 1999 Canadian GP)
Poles: 1
Fastest laps: 1
Points: .49
Honours: . . . .1994 ITALIAN FORMULA THREE CHAMPION & MONACO FORMULA THREE GP WINNER, 1991 EUROPEAN KART RUNNER-UP

Giancarlo Fisichella won't look back on 1999 with any great fondness. For, as in 1998, he ended the year ninth overall. And, as in 1998, his season started with promise, then tailed away. Indeed, Giancarlo never scored again after achieving his best result in the sixth of the 16 Grands Prix.

The chief problem was Benetton's chassis, one that offered no grip, either with or without its supposedly groundbreaking FTT system.

Giancarlo started with fourth in the Australian GP. When the next three races yielded a pair of fifths, matters didn't seem too bad. But they were largely the result of the drivers from the other top teams retiring. Indeed, it was misleading to think of Benetton as a top team anymore. And, save for a

fortuitous second place in the Canadian Grand Prix, the midfield was where it belonged.

There was one opportunity to make amends, and this was when Giancarlo found himself leading the wet/dry European Grand Prix at the Nurburgring. But he, like David Coulthard before him, slid off the track when leading and was out. So, will Giancarlo be able to do better this year? Unless the latest Supertec engine is streets better than last year's, the answer is probably no.

An Italian hotshot

Karting was where Giancarlo made his name before he moved to cars in 1991 with a year in Formula Alfa Boxer. Three years in Italian Formula Three followed. Having finished as runner-up in 1993, he won the title in 1994 and the Monaco Formula Three race. Unable to afford to progress to Formula 3000 for 1995, Giancarlo was snapped up by Alfa Romeo for the International Touring Car Championship. Giancarlo spent two successful years in this high-tech arena, but was more interested in single-seaters. Test driver for Minardi in 1995, he made his Formula One debut for them in 1996, contesting eight races before being replaced by rentadriver Giovanni Lavaggi.

Eddie Jordan signed him for 1997, and Giancarlo rewarded him by placing eighth overall, with a best result of second in the Belgian Grand Prix after leading the German

Grand Prix. Giancarlo loved the team but was forced to move to Benetton in 1998 after losing a court case that ruled that he was bound by a management contract.

Life at Benetton was kind to him, though, with the calming influence of David Richards helping Giancarlo to mature. However, it became clear that Bridgestone's efforts were behind McLaren and not Benetton. And, after finishing second at Monaco and Montreal, the team's drop from competitiveness was obvious. However, Giancarlo made the most of a wet but drying track to grab pole for the Austrian Grand Prix, but he slipped down the order and ended the year ninth overall, four places ahead of team-mate Alexander Wurz.

ALEXANDER WURZ

IN NEED OF A GOOD CAR

Alexander Wurz was almost invisible through the 1999 season, which is difficult for a man of his lofty stature. But unless Benetton gives him a better car this year, it is easy to see the lanky Austrian slipping from Formula One.

TRACK NOTES

Nationality: . . . . .AUSTRIAN
Born: . . . . . . .FEBRUARY 15, 1974,
. . . . .WAITHOFEN, AUSTRIA
Teams: . . . . . .BENETTON 1997–2000

Career record

First Grand Prix: . .1997 CANADIAN GP
Grand Prix starts: 35
Grand Prix wins: . . . . .NONE
(best result: third, 1997 British GP)
Poles: . . . . .NONE
Fastest laps: . . . . .NONE
Points: 24
Honours: . . .1996 LE MANS 24 HOURS
WINNER, 1994 GERMAN FORMULA
THREE RUNNER-UP, 1993 AUSTRIAN
FORMULA THREE CHAMPION,
1992 GERMAN & AUSTRIAN FORMULA
FORD CHAMPION

LOOKING FOR GRIP: Alexander Wurz had a hard time of things last year and is looking to save his career

There is no way that Alexander Wurz can have enjoyed last season. After all, he scored 17 points in his first full season in 1998 and yet came away with just three points last year. However, the blame for this must rest on the shoulders of a Benetton chassis that offered little grip. The relative lack of power from the team's Playlife engines could also be touted as an excuse, except for the fact that Ralf Schumacher had one in his Williams and scored 35 points.

The damage done to Alexander's reputation is not so easy to explain away, especially as he qualified ahead of team-mate Giancarlo Fisichella only three times in 16 Grands Prix, and finished ahead of him only once on the road. Alexander's points came from sixth place at Monaco and fifth, fittingly, in Austria, with Fisichella outscoring him by ten points.

So this season is going to be critical and both Alexander and Giancarlo must be praying that Benetton's design team has produced something special over the winter. They must also be praying that Renault decides to make its return to Formula One and renews its acquaintance with the team with a works engine deal for 2001.

From two wheels to four

Despite his great stature, Alexander was always going to be involved in motor sport in some manner, as both his father and his grandfather used to compete. However, Alexander cut his teeth in BMX cycle racing rather than karting, becoming world champion. But car racing followed and Alexander won the German and Austrian Formula Ford titles in 1992. Three seasons of Formula Three followed, with his best being the middle one when he was runner-up in the German series. He landed a drive in the International Touring Car series with Opel for 1996. But his highlight was winning the Le Mans 24 Hours at his first attempt, and he stuck with sportscars in 1997 by being a race-winning member of the Mercedes GT team.

The 1997 season also gave him his Formula One break, subbing at Benetton for Berger. Starting at the Canadian Grand Prix, he raced strongly before retiring from sixth. He impressed further by outqualifying team-mate Jean Alesi at Magny-Cours. But he impressed most of all by trailing Alesi throughout the British Grand Prix en route to third place. Then Berger recovered from sinus problems and Alexander reverted to his role in Benetton's test team.

Although Alexander seemed to move easily on to Fisichella's pace in 1998, he never made it to the podium, finishing fourth five times before the team began to struggle as Williams and Jordan found their feet.

SAUBER

REQUIRING SOME IMPETUS

Sauber never seems to shine. Jean Alesi failed to take it to new heights and has left, to be replaced by Mika Salo who will be hoping he will be the man to propel the team into the limelight.

I wrote last year that there's something about Sauber that suggests that it will never really cut it in Formula One. Twelve months on and there is no evidence to the contrary. Indeed, Sauber scored even fewer points than it did in 1998 and the only moments that stick in the memory were Jean Alesi running third in the deluge at Magny-Cours before falling off, and Pedro Diniz flipping and removing his rollhoop at the Nurburgring.

EVERY SECOND COUNTS: Sauber's pitcrew demonstrate their Swiss precision

THE VIPs

Peter Sauber

This former sportscar racer moved almost effortlessly to become a constructor. The success of his cars led to Mercedes making Sauber its racing department in 1988, winning the world sportscar title and the Le Mans 24 Hours in 1989. Mercedes helped Sauber graduate to Formula One in 1993, but he's had to fend for himself since 1995.

Osamu Goto

One of the strongest parts of the Sauber equation is its engines and the man in charge of this is Osamu. He was the brain behind Honda's title-winning spell in Formula One through the 1980s, then moved from Honda to McLaren in 1991 and on to Ferrari to run its engine programme in 1994. When Sauber started using Petronas-badged Ferrari engines in 1997, he became head of the team's engine department.

FOR THE RECORD

Country of origin: ....Switzerland
Team base: ....Hinwil, Switzerland
Date of formation: 1970
Active years in Formula One: ....From 1993
Grands Prix contested: 113
Wins: ....None
Pole positions: ....None
Fastest laps: ....None

Drivers and Results 1999

Driver	Nationality	Races	Wins	Pts	Pos
Jean Alesi	French	16	0	2	15th
Pedro Diniz	Brazilian	16	0	3	13th

Car specifications

Sponsors: ....Red Bull, Petronas Malaysia
Team principal: ....Peter Sauber
Team manager: ....Beat Zehnder
Designer: ....Leo Ress
Chief engineer: ....Gabriele delli Colli
Test driver: ....Enrique Bernoldi
Chassis: ....Sauber C19
Engine: ....Petronas V10

calls over his radio to visit the pits... This hastened his decision to move to Prost for 2000.

Diniz is staying for 2000, joined by Mika Salo. It's not clear who is expected to become team leader, but the two raced together without problem at Arrows in 1998 when there were no clear team orders. Diniz had wavered about staying on during last season, but was convinced by Peter Sauber that technical changes were afoot and agreed to stay. He must be hoping that the latest Ferrari engine – badged as a Petronas, of course – will be harnessed to a chassis that is worthy of it. Again, for Sauber to progress, it must start testing more.

Groomed by Mercedes

Sauber began its life long before it broke into Formula One in 1993, as the team was formed back in 1970 to concentrate on sportscar racing. Sauber's fortunes picked up when it helped Mercedes to win both the Le Mans 24 Hours and the World Sportscar Championship in 1989. Graduating to Formula One in 1993 with Mercedes-sourced Ilmor engines, the team scored on its debut when JJ Lehto finished fifth in the South African Grand Prix. He and Karl Wendlinger then each scored a fourth place. Wendlinger crashed at Monaco in 1994 and fell into a three-week coma, while Lehto had made way for Heinz-Harald Frentzen who finished third in the 1995 Italian Grand Prix. This result was all the more impressive as Sauber lost its support from Mercedes when they took their engines to McLaren, and Sauber had to make do with customer Ford engines. Persevering with Ford power in 1996, Frentzen was joined by Johnny Herbert, who he outscored, but Herbert produced the best result with third at Monaco.

Ford power made way for Ferrari horses in 1997, with Herbert leading the line-up. But he was knocked out of the first race at the first corner and his season got little better until he was rewarded with third in the Hungarian Grand Prix. Jean Alesi arrived with great expectation in 1998 and soon displaced Herbert as the driver behind whom the team was putting its weight. Indeed, it was a terrible year for Herbert as he scored just once. Alesi fared better as he assumed the mantle of team leader, scoring four times, including a surprise third place at Spa-Francorchamps.

At the time, I mused that the lack of success was because the team comes from a country with no racing history or motor sport industry infrastructure. Or maybe that its budget wasn't enough to match the amount of testing undertaken by the top teams. But, whatever, with the 1998-spec Ferrari engines in their tails, the cars should have achieved far more than five sixth-place finishes.

On top of that, because the cars were good enough generally to stay on the lead lap or be lapped just the once, they featured on the world's television screens even less than the oft-lapped 'Tail End Charlies' from Minardi and Arrows.

The year gone by

If Sauber started 1999 with two main challenges, then it failed in one and just about succeeded in the other. The failure came in its inability to score its first Grand Prix win in its seventh season. The success came in that Sauber appeared to run two cars to the same level for the first time. However, this was at too low a level to yield many points towards its Constructors' Cup tally. Indeed, Sauber slipped from sixth overall in 1998 to eighth.

As has often been the case in Alesi's career, he brought his car home to the finish more times than his team-mate, but sixth was his best result. This wasn't exceeded by Diniz, but the Brazilian finished sixth on each of his three finishes alongside his 11 retirements in the first 14 rounds. Alesi's low point was when memories of Melbourne 1997 came flooding back when he ran out of fuel in the Austrian Grand Prix after failing to hear

SWISS SMOKESCREEN: Team owner Peter Sauber confounds the saying 'close, but no cigar' as he chews on Cuba's finest in a year when his team failed to shine

PEDRO DINIZ

TREADING WATER

Pedro Diniz is now accepted as a driver in his own right, rather than just as a rentadriver, but staying on for a second year with Sauber is not necessarily considered to be the best way to progress and to go for that first win.

TRACK NOTES

Nationality: . . . . .BRAZILIAN
Born: . . . . .MAY 22, 1970,
. . . . .SAO PAULO, BRAZIL
Teams: . . . . . . .FORTI CORSE 1995,
. . . . .LIGIER 1996,
. . . . .ARROWS 1997–1998,
. . . . .SAUBER 1999–2000

Career record

First Grand Prix: .1995 BRAZILIAN GP
Starts: 82
Wins: . . . . .NONE
*(best result: fifth in 1997 Luxembourg
GP and 1998 Belgian GP)*
Pole positions: . . . . .NONE
Fastest laps: . . . . .NONE
Points: 10
Honours: . . . . .NONE

PONDERING HIS DECISION: Unhappy with progress in 1999, Pedro Diniz will be hoping that Sauber advances

Compare the scores: Pedro Diniz, three points, Jean Alesi, two. Neither of these 1999 tallies is impressive – Sauber had a far from impressive season. The important fact, though, is that Pedro outscored his more illustrious team-mate, a driver respected for his ability to score points.

However, while Alesi showed his frustration with the Swiss team's lack of progress and quit to join Prost for this year, Pedro has elected to stay for a second season. This isn't to say that he didn't have his doubts about Sauber's direction. But team boss Peter Sauber convinced Pedro that development plans were in place and so he elected to stay.

Compare Pedro's qualifying rankings with Alesi's and the French driver came out ahead, beating the Brazilian on 12 of the 16 occasions and producing a few stunning race performances. However, these invariably led to disappointment. Not that Pedro enjoyed much in the way of results, finishing just four times, and scoring a point a time for sixth place in three of these. So, it was a season that Pedro will largely want to forget, apart from that part about outscoring his team-mate...

This season will see Pedro reunited with Mika Salo, his team-mate at Arrows in 1998. Pedro will be anxious to show that not only can he outscore Alesi, but also have a go at outscoring Salo, a driver seen in a different light since he twice finished on the podium for Ferrari when he was a stand-in. For the record, they scored three points apiece in 1998.

Looking at the equipment, Sauber should have a healthy helping of horsepower, as they will again be racing with Ferrari's engines from the previous year – badged as Petronas engines in deference to the team's sponsor. And these are reported to have pushed out 840bhp at the end of last year.

The real deal

Encouraged into the sport by his father, who'd been a racer in his day, Pedro raced in Formula Ford and Formula Three before coming to Britain in 1991 to race alongside Rubens Barrichello at West Surrey Racing. His second season of British Formula Three yielded two third places, before Pedro moved up to Formula 3000, spending two years with Forti. There was the odd good result, but Pedro was seen as a driver making the most of his family's supermarket millions. Indeed, these were put to good use to move to Formula One with Forti. But the team spent its first year woefully off the pace in 1995 and Pedro opted to join Ligier instead in 1996, making people take notice by occasionally outracing team-mate Olivier Panis. It was the same story with Damon Hill at Arrows in 1997. And still Pedro is proving himself!

MIKA SALO

BACK ON BOARD

Mika Salo started last year without a drive, stood in for two teams, showed his skills by leading the German Grand Prix for Ferrari, and is now back with a fulltime drive, albeit with the less than fancied Sauber team.

British Formula Three in 1989, losing out in a season-long battle with Hakkinen in 1990. While Hakkinen leapt to Formula One, Mika lacked a budget and headed for Japanese Formula 3000 where he took several years to land a competitive drive.

Mika made it to Formula One at the end of 1994 when he did a great job for the dying Lotus team. Signed by Tyrrell, he ran third in the first Grand Prix of 1995, in Brazil, before suffering cramp that forced him to spin back to seventh. Despite this showing, Mika scored on only three occasions.

The Tyrrell chassis was considerably better in 1996, but all too often they pulled off with engine failures. And 1997 was little better. A move to Arrows in 1998 led to flashes of ability, but these were all too often disguised by the car's woeful lack of power and poor reliability. However, as in 1997, he dragged his underpowered car into the points at Monaco with a faultless drive.

TRACK NOTES

Nationality: . . . . .FINNISH
Born: . . . . .30 NOVEMBER 1966,
. . . . .HELSINKI, FINLAND
Teams: . . . . .LOTUS 1994,
. . . . .TYRRELL 1995–1997,
. . . . .ARROWS 1998,
. . . . .BAR 1999,
. . . . .FERRARI 1999,
. . . . .SAUBER 2000

Career record

First Grand Prix: . .1994 JAPANESE GP
Grand Prix starts: 77
Grand Prix wins: . . . . .NONE
(best result: second, 1999 German GP)
Poles: . . . . .NONE
Fastest laps: . . . . .NONE
Points: 25
Honours: . . .1990 BRITISH FORMULA
THREE RUNNER-UP, 1988 EUROPEAN
FORMULA FORD CHAMPION

At the beginning of last year, Mika Salo was out of a drive, having been edged out of his seat at Arrows as the team went through ownership turmoil. Twelve months on, he has a firm contract in his pocket and is reunited with his 1998 Arrows team-mate Pedro Diniz at Sauber. The difference is that he has driven for two teams in the intervening period and has even experienced leading the German Grand Prix for Ferrari.

Mika was called into action by British American Racing when Ricardo Zonta injured himself at the Brazilian Grand Prix. This gave the Finn a three-race run as his replacement, even giving the troubled new team its first finish. Mika then focused on 2000 until Michael Schumacher broke his right leg in the British Grand Prix. By the time his stand-in period was over, he'd raced six times and finished second at Hockenheim and third at Monza. Mika's form fluctuated though, and the good he did in one race was often undone by his form in the next. However, with balanced employment, expect Mika to settle down at Sauber. He will at least be used to the engine, as although this will be badged as a Petronas, it's the one he used at Ferrari last year. However, it's extremely unlikely that the Swiss team will provide him with the equipment he needs to try to prove that it is he who is the best Finnish driver.

Mika versus Mika

Mika raced against sworn rival Mika Hakkinen in karts, then followed him into cars, winning the 1988 European Formula Ford title ahead of Michael Schumacher. He joined Hakkinen in

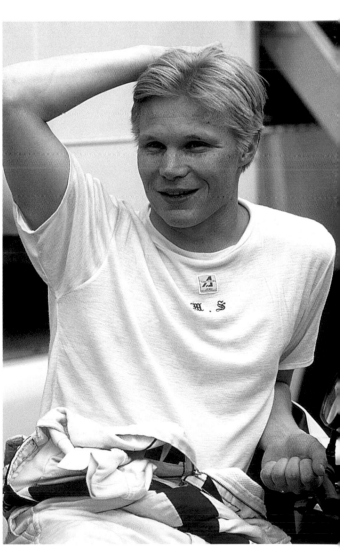

LAIDBACK FINN: Mika Salo always appears relaxed, but he's deadly serious about establishing his name

PROST

CHASING ITS FIRST WIN

Last season appeared to be a lost one for Prost, with little in the way of results, a disagreement with its engine supplier and its better driver leaving. But second place at the European Grand Prix calmed nerves and now Jean Alesi is the team's new number one.

When Alain Prost's team scored only one point in 1998 in its second season since the four-time World Champion had taken it over from Ligier, Alain wasn't happy. Indeed, it was not until four races before season's end that Jarno Trulli picked up this solitary point at Spa-Francorchamps, this crucial point that earned the team its travel money for 1999. The team would have to do far better, Alain said. And, looking at their season-ending tally of nine points, they did do better. But it still wasn't what Alain was looking for.

Alain had retained his 1998 driver line-up, with Trulli seen by many as the team's number one and long-time servant Olivier Panis reduced to the role of supporting driver. Peugeot was still

LOOKING AHEAD: Team boss Alain Prost has his sights set on a win

FOR THE RECORD

Country of origin: . . . . .France
Team base: .Guyancourt, France
Date of formation: .1971 (as Ligier)
Active years in Formula One: . . . . .From 1976
Grands Prix contested: 375
Wins: 9
Pole positions: 9
Fastest laps: 11

Drivers and Results 1999

Driver	Nationality	Races	Wins	Pts	Pos
Olivier Panis	French	16	0	2	15th
Jarno Trulli	Italian	16	0	7	11th

Car specifications

Sponsors: . . . . .Gauloises, Alcatel, LV Capital
Team principal: . . . . .Alain Prost
Team manager: . . . . .Jean-Pierre Chatanet
Designers: . . . . .John Barnard, Alan Jenkins
Chief engineer: . . . . .Vincent Gaillardot
Test driver: . . . . .tba
Chassis: . . . . .Prost AP03
Engine: . . . . .Peugeot V10

New for 2000

Looking ahead to this season, there are three new ingredients. First off, Alan Jenkins has been drafted onto the design force, having been out of a job since leaving Stewart following the arrival from Jordan of Gary Anderson. Judging by the performance of the Stewart chassis last year, which was almost all Jenkins's work, the team has done well from this. Add to this the fact that Prost himself has an excellent relationship with Alan from their days together at McLaren, when they worked in a triangle with Barnard that has now been reunited, and this bodes well. Racing for the glory of France can wait, as, for now, Prost simply wants success. Turning it into all-French success can follow.

From Ligier to Prost

To understand the Prost team, one must know the history of Ligier. This wholly-French team made its Formula One debut in 1976 under the guidance of former rugby star and occasional 1960s Grand Prix driver Guy Ligier. Jacques Laffite scored its first win in the Swedish Grand Prix in 1977 and three more wins followed in the first five races of the 1979 season, with Laffite scoring the first two and Patrick Depailler the third. But this early season advantage was not built upon and Ferrari drivers controlled the year. The next two seasons yielded two wins, with Laffite and Didier Pironi taking one each in 1980 and Laffite taking both in 1981. But the team slid from competitiveness and it wasn't until 1996 that it won again, thanks to a superb drive by Olivier Panis in the wet at Monaco. Its final years were tortured ones as Prost had a bid to take the team over turned down in 1992 when it passed instead to Cyril de Rouvre. But de Rouvre was jailed for fraud and Benetton boss Flavio Briatore took over in 1994. Tom Walkinshaw then took control in 1996, but sold out and went to Arrows, finally leaving the way clear for Prost to take over for 1997.

ESTABLISHED REPUTATION: John Barnard is a designer of the highest order, who designed the chassis with which Alain Prost raced to his three World Championship titles with McLaren. So they know each other extremely well

on board to supply the engines, and the whole Prost operation was now safely established in its new base at Guyancourt near Paris. Race wins weren't expected, but regular points scores were. When neither driver managed to qualify in the top ten for the first three Grands Prix, it became clear that the combination wasn't up to the job. Although Panis had scored a point at the Brazilian Grand Prix, it was Trulli who looked the stronger, qualifying in the top ten for the next four races and finishing sixth in the Spanish Grand Prix. Mind you, a well-timed run in torrential rain in qualifying for the French Grand Prix saw Panis qualify third. But the race was also a lottery and he slipped back to eighth, one place behind Trulli.

At this point Prost's future with Peugeot was looking shaky, with Alain pushing the automotive giant to confirm its technical development plans and threatening to source his engines from elsewhere if they couldn't confirm that they would take the battle to the other engine suppliers. However, their relationship settled down again just when it looked as though divorce was imminent. And, with such a scarcity of works engine deals available, this must have come as a relief.

A little relief was provided when Panis picked up another point in the German Grand Prix, but this was nothing next to the relief felt at the European Grand Prix when both drivers made the most of the changing weather conditions and Trulli collected the team's best result in its Prost era, second place between the two Stewarts. Panis felt that he too should have been in the points, as he started from fifth on the grid, but guessed wrong on tyres.

JEAN ALESI

JOINING A FRIEND

Jean Alesi has turned his back on a year of frustration with Sauber to join forces with former team-mate and good friend Alain Prost, desperate to spring one last surprise.

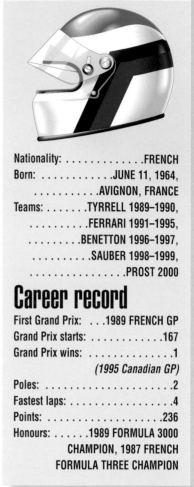

TRACK NOTES

Nationality:	FRENCH
Born:	JUNE 11, 1964, AVIGNON, FRANCE
Teams:	TYRRELL 1989–1990, FERRARI 1991–1995, BENETTON 1996–1997, SAUBER 1998–1999, PROST 2000

Career record

First Grand Prix:	1989 FRENCH GP
Grand Prix starts:	167
Grand Prix wins:	1
	(1995 Canadian GP)
Poles:	2
Fastest laps:	4
Points:	236
Honours:	1989 FORMULA 3000 CHAMPION, 1987 FRENCH FORMULA THREE CHAMPION

A POINT TO PROVE: Jean Alesi doesn't like being the old man of Formula One and is anxious to show that he has another win in him

With Damon Hill's retirement, Jean Alesi is now the old man of Formula One – by 16 days from Johnny Herbert – but his enthusiasm for racing marks him out as one of the ones to watch. Indeed, Jean cares little for matters outside the cockpit, and simply wants to be out in a racing car. For fans of spectacular driving, you should long for this to be on a wet track...

For the new season, he will be more charged up than ever, joining forces with former Ferrari team-mate and firm friend Alain Prost. If Peugeot produces a better engine to go with what could be a very tidy chassis from John Barnard and Alan Jenkins, then there's no reason why Jean shouldn't deliver in 2000. Particularly in the wet.

A mixed history

Jean burst onto the scene midway through 1989, finishing fourth for Tyrrell on his debut in the French Grand Prix. He will ever be remembered for his wonderful dice for the lead with Ayrton Senna at Phoenix the following year. Then came a five-year spell with Ferrari, a team not producing of its best during that period. Frequent flashes of brilliance resulted, though, in just one win, in Canada in 1995. Two years at Benetton followed from 1996, but his relationship with team boss Flavio Briatore was never less than fiery.

In 1998, Jean moved to Sauber where he failed to get on with team-mate Herbert. But, Ferrari engines withstanding, there was little to get excited about, save for inspired moments such as just failing to give Sauber its first pole position at the Austrian Grand Prix when he was pipped by Giancarlo Fisichella's Benetton in the dying seconds on a drying track. However, he peaked with third place at the accident-strewn Belgian Grand Prix.

The 1999 season was even more frustrating. Indeed, Jean threw in the towel as early as the Hungarian Grand Prix, a race in which his car ran out of fuel on three occasions… Indeed, up to this time he'd only scored one point for sixth place at the San Marino Grand Prix. So, he was only too delighted when Prost snapped up his services.

Whatever his motivation out of the car, Jean is always a trier in the cockpit, invariably finishing more races than any team-mate. This was true again and he rounded out the year with sixth place at the Suzuka finale. However, he was outscored, three to two, by team-mate Pedro Diniz, which must have left memories of strong drives in Brazil and France that produced nothing gnawing away at him.

But, rest assured, Jean will be firing on all cylinders again for a new challenge with Prost.

NICK HEIDFELD

MOVING UP A GEAR

Groomed by Mercedes, a strong test driver for McLaren and a dominant Formula 3000 champion, Nick Heidfeld has been given his Formula One break by Prost and the German is worth watching as a star in the making.

Nick Heidfeld is a rare new face in Formula One for 2000, but he is no stranger to a Formula One cockpit. The reason for this is that he has been groomed for stardom by Mercedes since his days in Formula Three. Indeed, Nick has been McLaren's test driver for the past two years, putting in a great deal of useful test mileage. And, it must be said, a lot of this has been at a good pace too, matching that of the team's regular drivers, Mika Hakkinen and David Coulthard.

With no ride opening up for him as the Finn and the Scot were retained, it was decided by Mercedes and McLaren to place Nick with another team so that he can add some Grand Prix experience to his testing miles. To this end, Alain Prost, a long-time friend of McLaren, has offered him his team's second seat alongside Jean Alesi. And, providing Nick does well, perhaps McLaren will open their doors to him in the future.

One thing that's for certain is that the fresh-faced German is ready for a new challenge after two years of Formula 3000. And the other thing that's for certain is his skill behind the wheel. With Prost at the helm running the French team in an international way, Nick should make useful progress, especially if Alesi also tries to help him in a master/apprentice way. It will, though, be Nick's first season away from Mercedes control, so it will certainly be an education.

Groomed for stardom

Like all the top drivers today, Nick was a hotshot in karting before progressing to Formula Ford as soon as he was old enough to be allowed to do so. That was in 1994 when he turned 17, and Nick dominated the FF1600 subclass of the German Formula Ford series. He was then runner-up in the main championship the following year. But it was in Formula Three that Nick made his name. Driving for Bertram Schafer Racing in 1996, Nick came on strong to win three races in a row towards the end of the season and ended up third overall in a season in which Jarno Trulli was a dominant champion.

However, 1997 was better and Nick won a tight battle with Timo Scheider to be crowned champion and land Mercedes backing which placed him with the McLaren junior team in Formula 3000 for 1998. And this he nearly won at his first attempt, winning three races and losing out narrowly to Juan Pablo Montoya. With no openings in Formula One for 1999, Nick had to stay on for a second season and did the only thing he could do to keep his momentum from stalling: he won the title in style.

TRACK NOTES

Nationality: . . . . .GERMAN
Born: . . . . .MAY 10, 1977
.MOENCHENGLADBACH, GERMANY
Teams: . . . . .PROST 2000

Career record
First Grand Prix: AUSTRALIAN GP 2000
Starts: . . . . .NONE
Wins: . . . . .NONE
Pole positions: . . . . .NONE
Fastest laps: . . . . .NONE
Points: . . . . .NONE
Honours: . . . . . .1999 FORMULA 3000
CHAMPION; 1998 FORMULA 3000
RUNNER-UP; 1997 GERMAN FORMULA
THREE CHAMPION; 1995 GERMAN
FORMULA FORD RUNNER-UP; 1994
GERMAN FF1600 CHAMPION

GERMANY'S NEW HOPE: Nick Heidfeld is likely to impress after a strong grounding in Formula 3000

ARROWS

LOOKING FOR A BOOST

THE VIPs

Mike Coughlan

Arrows' technical director trained as a student with Rolls Royce before joining Tiga Racing Cars, designing everything from Formula Fords to Group C sportscars. His first foray into Formula One was with Lotus, leaving in 1990 to join Benetton. He moved via Tyrrell to Ferrari before joining Arrows in 1997.

Tom Walkinshaw

This Scot is a formidable character, a man with a rugby prop forward's physique that belies the fact that he used to race single-seaters before turning successfully to touring cars. As a team chief, he brought huge success to Jaguar in sportscars, then moved to Formula One with Benetton in 1994. He then took over Ligier before taking control of Arrows in 1997.

Arrows will be hoping that its move to Supertec power will be what moves it up the Grand Prix starting grids in 2000. However, a lack of budget means a relative lack of testing and that inevitably spells failure.

The greatest leap forward for Arrows looking ahead to the first Formula One World Championship of the 21st century is that the team will no longer be using its "home-grown" engines that left its drivers struggling with a crippling lack of horsepower in recent years. For the season ahead, Arrows has a deal to run Supertec engines. This is clearly good news, especially as the new Supertec engine promises to be better than the 1999 version. However, the bad news is that this deal won't necessarily ensure Arrows will move away from its back-of-the-grid battle with Minardi, as the Italian team has also landed a deal to use better engines.

There is altogether more positive news on the chassis front, though, as drivers Pedro de la Rosa and Toranosuke Takagi won't have to make do with a chassis updated from the previous season, as happened last year. No, for this year, Mike Coughlan and his crew have started with a "clean sheet of paper". All Arrows fans will be praying that the difference is obvious. However, the team will have to raise the money to go testing, as no team extracts the maximum from its chassis without testing every bit as much as its rivals.

De la Rosa had a dream Formula One debut by scoring a point in the opening round at Melbourne last year. Mind you, this had more to do with the frontrunners retiring than with a startling turn of pace. Indeed, Arrows required just one more car to hit trouble and it would have had Takagi in the points as well, as he finished seventh.

Sadly, that was the only point Arrows scored all year. But at least it was one more point than British American Racing scored, so Arrows will have that all-important travel money from the FIA for this year.

It wasn't just a lack of speed that troubled the Arrows drivers, but a lack of reliability, with both racking up 11 retirements apiece, although Takagi didn't help himself on occasion by becoming involved in accidents. However, with Mika Salo having been dropped from the Arrows line-up just before the opening race, neither driver had a yardstick for their performance.

SERIOUS BUSINESS: Arrows boss Tom Walkinshaw shows that being at the back of the grid is no laughing matter

FOR THE RECORD

Country of origin:	England
Team base:	Witney, England
Founded:	1977
Active in Formula One:	From 1978
Grands Prix contested:	337
Grand Prix wins:	None
Pole positions:	None
Fastest laps:	None

Drivers and Results 1999

Driver	Nationality	Races	Wins	Pts	Pos
Pedro de la Rosa	Spanish	16	0	1	17th
Toranosuke Takagi	Japanese	16	0	0	N/A

Car specifications

Sponsors:	Repsol, Baan, PIAA
Team principal:	Tom Walkinshaw
Team manager:	Rod Benoist
Designer:	Mike Coughlan
Chief engineer:	Chris Dyer
Test driver:	tba
Chassis:	Arrows A21
Engine:	Supertec V10

Broken promises

The biggest problem between the 1998 season and last season was that Arrows was desperate for financial assistance and spent the close-season chasing a backer. With less than three months to go before the first race of the season it seemed as though the Zakspeed sportscar team would be Walkinshaw's new partner. But the German team failed to clinch the deal that would see it return to Formula One for the first time since 1989. And, with a month or so to go before the first race a new face burst onto the Grand Prix scene: Malik Ido Ibrahim.

The Nigerian described people in Formula One as "pussycats", people that someone with his financial background would be able to jump to his tune. Yet, he had parted company with the team before the season was out as he'd failed to produce the funding that the team needed so desperately. Those who watched the countdown sign-writing on the sides of the black and orange cars noted that the appointed countdown day came and went without the announcement of a big sponsor to save the team. Soon afterwards, Malik launched the "t-minus" range of products, but this seemed the act of someone shutting the stable door after the horse had bolted. The big one had got away. And Arrows spent the winter of 1999–2000 chasing after money again.

A fruitless pursuit

Arrows holds the sad record that it has contested more Grands Prix without a win than any other team. And that record now stands at 337, with the next least successful team being Minardi with 237. However, on two occasions in the team's past it looked as though the wait would be brought to an end. Ironically, the first of these came in only its second race when Riccardo Patrese threatened to win the 1978 South African GP. Then, in 1997, Damon Hill's failing Arrows was overhauled by Jacques Villeneuve half a lap from the end of the Hungarian GP and limped home second. Apart from that, the cupboard is bare.

THE MEN IN BLACK: Despite their drivers seldom being in a position to score points in 1999, the Arrows pitcrew still gave of their best in those mid-race pit stops

PEDRO DE LA ROSA

ANXIOUS FOR HORSEPOWER

Pedro de la Rosa scored on his Formula One debut last year. And this was with Arrows. However, that was to prove his only point and he will be desperate for Arrows to make strides so that he can be in the points again.

A MATURE SHOWING: Pedro de la Rosa lived up to his reputation by scoring on his Formula One debut in Melbourne, but his maiden season was riddled with retirements

Pedro's deal with Arrows was a last-minute affair, landed thanks to his healthy backing from Spanish petrochemical company Repsol, displacing Mika Salo. However, this is to sell Pedro short, as this was merely a reflection of Arrows' shortage of money, as his skills behind the wheel were widely recognized after a year of testing for Jordan.

Pedro's ability was rewarded first time out, when he finished sixth in the Australian Grand Prix. Admittedly it was a race in which most drivers retired, but he finished on the lead lap, just ahead of team-mate Toranosuke Takagi, for what was to prove the only point Arrows would score all year. And it proved to be a vital point, as it was this that guaranteed the team travel money for this year.

Pedro is a thinking driver, one who will bring the car home. However, he showed that he has good speed over one lap too when he matched Takagi eight-all in qualifying, an area that is the Japanese driver's strength.

Pedro is enthused by the fact that Arrows has traded up from its own engines to ones from Supertec for this year. And, not only ought these offer more horsepower, but also superior reliability which will be welcome indeed, as Pedro finished only four times in 16 races last year.

Taking the eastern route

Known by his full name of Pedro Martinez de la

TRACK NOTES

Nationality: . . . . .SPANISH
Born: . . . . . . .FEBRUARY 24, 1971,
. . . . .BARCELONA, SPAIN
Teams: . . . . . .ARROWS 1999–2000

Career record
First Grand Prix: 1999 AUSTRALIAN GP
Grand Prix starts: 16
Grand Prix wins: . . . . .NONE
Poles: . . . . .NONE
Fastest laps: . . . . .NONE
Points: .1
Honours: . . . .1998 FORMULA NIPPON
CHAMPION, 1995 ALL-JAPAN
FORMULA THREE CHAMPION, 1992
EUROPEAN & BRITISH FORMULA
RENAULT CHAMPION, 1990 SPANISH
FORMULA FORD CHAMPION

Rosa when he came to Britain to compete in Formula Ford and then in Formula Renault in the early 1990s, he was backed by Racing for Spain and used his obvious intelligence to good effect. His style was perfect for Formula Three, where a smooth approach pays. But the choice of an uncompetitive Renault engine wasted his second season in the category, in 1994, the year in which Jan Magnussen dominated with a Mugen Honda.

Pedro couldn't afford a third season in British Formula Three. So he signed for the TOM'S team and dominated the Japanese series in 1995. Thus he graduated to Formula Nippon, winning the title at his second attempt with the crack Nova Engineering team by taking six wins from ten starts.

S pain had been desperate for years to have a home-grown driver to go with its Grand Prix. And Pedro de la Rosa was long seen as that man. Amazingly, just like waiting for a bus, when he made the step last year, he was joined by compatriot Marc Gene. Indeed, they spent much of the year fighting at the back of the grid. But it was the more experienced Pedro who held the upper hand, even though they came away from the season with a point apiece.

TORANOSUKE TAKAGI

JAPAN STILL EXPECTS

Toranosuke Takagi impressed in his first year of Formula One and was expected to start scoring points last year. However, driving for Arrows seldom yields points, and there's no reason to think 2000 will be any different.

Having spent his first year in Formula One with the ailing Tyrrell team in 1998, Toranosuke Takagi came out of it with a reputation for speed but also one for mistakes. Moving to Arrows last year saw him driving for a team that was more secure but even less competitive. Sadly, this meant that onlookers saw less of the speed from the mercurial Japanese driver and more retirements. Not all of these were Toranosuke's fault, but by the end of the year he was slipping back into his bad old ways. The outcome was no points and his reputation as Japan's bright new thing starting to slip.

The season started brightly enough as Toranosuke scored his best ever result, seventh place at the Australian Grand Prix, one place behind team-mate Pedro de la Rosa. However, that was to be his highest placing of the year, with eighth in the second race at Interlagos his next best. Trouble was, that meant that he was seventh out of eight finishers in Australia and eighth out of nine in Brazil.

The season went downhill from there as he struggled with a lack of horsepower from the Arrows-built engines and with a chassis that was only an update of the 1998 chassis. Toranosuke finished on only three more occasions, never finishing in the top ten again and, on top of this, then being disqualified from the French Grand Prix.

So, it's not surprising that other teams haven't thrown open their doors to Toranosuke, not that there have been many drives up for grabs. However, for his second year with Arrows, Toranosuke can at least look forward to more horsepower as Tom Walkinshaw has done a deal for Supertec engines. Trouble is, rivals Minardi will also be using more powerful engines, so they could yet be renewing their scrap to get off the back row of the grid. An all new chassis should also help Toranosuke's cause.

Help from above

Toranosuke's abilities were spotted by former Formula One driver Satoru Nakajima back in 1993

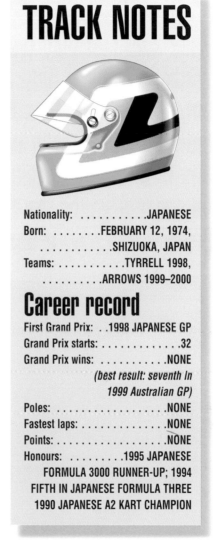

TRACK NOTES

Nationality: . . . . .JAPANESE
Born: . . . . .FEBRUARY 12, 1974,
. . . . .SHIZUOKA, JAPAN
Teams: . . . . .TYRRELL 1998,
. . . . .ARROWS 1999–2000

Career record

First Grand Prix: . .1998 JAPANESE GP
Grand Prix starts: 32
Grand Prix wins: . . . . .NONE
*(best result: seventh in
1999 Australian GP)*
Poles: . . . . .NONE
Fastest laps: . . . . .NONE
Points: . . . . .NONE
Honours: . . . . .1995 JAPANESE
FORMULA 3000 RUNNER-UP; 1994
FIFTH IN JAPANESE FORMULA THREE
1990 JAPANESE A2 KART CHAMPION

DESPERATE FOR POINTS: Toranosuke Takagi has yet to score a point after two full seasons of Formula One

and he signed him up to drive in his Formula Three team in 1994. He did well against the crop of overseas drivers who were dominating the Japanese championship and moved up to Nakajima's Formula Nippon team. Impressively, Toranosuke ended his first year in Japan's equivalent of Formula 3000 as runner-up. But he stayed on to try and win the title the following year when he came up against Ralf Schumacher and Norberto Fontana, with the German taking the title. By then, however, Nakajima had landed Toranosuke the Tyrrell test seat and he spent the year racing in the Porsche Supercup to learn the Grand Prix circuits of Europe.

BRITISH AMERICAN RACING HONDA

CHASING THE DREAM

They said that they would be Grand Prix winners in their first season of Formula One, but British American Racing came away from their maiden season with nothing. However, this is a team that will succeed. It will just take a few years, as it has the money, the drivers and now it has works Honda engines.

THE VIPs

Craig Pollock
Craig met Jacques Villeneuve when he coached him at skiing at school in Switzerland. He later chanced upon Jacques who asked him to help with his racing career and guided him from Japanese Formula Three to Toyota Atlantic, to Indycars and then Formula One. He then founded British American Racing and Jacques followed him there.

Malcolm Oastler
Australian racing car designer learned the sport from the driving seat in Formula Ford in Australia and then Britain before making his name with Reynard by penning chassis in Formula 3000 and Indycars with great success before being assigned the task of designing BAR's first Formula One car for last year.

MEETING OF MINDS: BAR number one Jacques Villeneuve has words with team principal Craig Pollock during the team's troubled first year

junior formulae, rather a team that was dreamt up by Craig Pollock and started at the top. This alone annoyed those who had earned their place in motor sport's pantheon. However, Pollock had chased the sponsorship and here they were. Trouble was, co-founder Adrian Reynard had predicted that they would win this first race, as Reynard cars had done when they moved into Formula Three, Formula 3000 and Indycars. Needless to say, Formula One is never that easy, and although Pollock had ameliorated this prediction to winning a race during the team's first year, he was still wide of the mark.

All the right ingredients

With a chassis designed by Malcolm Oastler, a second division engine from Supertec, a former World Champion in Villeneuve and a promising rookie in Ricardo Zonta, BAR looked to be starting out with a point-scoring capability. On

British American Racing arrived with much fanfare and yet failed to walk away from their maiden season of Formula One with a single point. Few teams have come away with so much egg on their faces. But this is to fail to comprehend how much harder it becomes to enter Formula One with every passing year.

What Jordan did in 1991 seems easy by comparison, as it takes so much money now to do things properly. And, whatever BAR did in 1999, it didn't cut corners.

Despite their promotional line of 'a tradition of excellence', BAR arrived from nowhere. It wasn't a team that had earned its stripes in the top of this, BAR had recruited people from almost every team in the pitlane, so there was experience aplenty. Yet, it never quite came together.

After all, for a driver of Villeneuve's experience and undoubted speed not to score even a single point is a clear sign of something not going right. And the answer to why he didn't score was not so much down to the speed of the car, rather to its reliability, as it took until the 12th round before he even finished a race… He seldom lost a point-scoring position when he retired, either.

The problems began in pre-season testing when vital parts, such as wings, fell off the cars. Endless other parts failed in the first half of the season. Every time it seemed to be something different. Then Zonta crashed in practice for his home race in Brazil and was out for three further Grands Prix while his foot injuries healed. Mika Salo replaced him and at least was classified seventh on his first outing at Imola, even if the car wasn't running when the flag fell. He recorded the team's first moving finish two races later when he was eighth in the Spanish Grand Prix. However, his drive was overshadowed by Villeneuve starting sixth and running third behind only the McLarens but ahead of the Ferraris. It all went wrong at his first pitstop and soon his gearbox failed, but the team had shown the form expected of it.

The problems led to the finding of a scapegoat, so team manager Greg Field parted company with BAR, his position being filled by Robert Synge. And still the results didn't come. It finally looked as though the first points were in the bag at the European Grand Prix, with Villeneuve running fifth with just five laps to go, but then his clutch failed.

Villeneuve can't be faulted for giving his all, with only the occasional outburst against the team, particularly against Reynard for not showing enough interest. Zonta was kept in his place and never troubled Villeneuve, although it's very likely that a team that failed to run its number one car successfully was never going to offer much hope to its clear number two.

Second time lucky?

For this year, though, the team will start with its structures in place, a year of vital experience behind it. But, most importantly, Pollock pulled off a huge coup by landing the works Honda engine deal, something that only became available when Honda decided not to return to Formula One with its own team. Not only did this put the noses of several leading teams out of joint, but it proved that Pollock really can talk a good game. His drivers won't be complaining either, as they will welcome the cutting of the power deficit of some 60bhp that they and other Supertec-powered teams were suffering to the likes of McLaren and Ferrari.

FOR THE RECORD

Country of origin:	England
Team base:	Brackley, England
Date of formation:	1999
Active years in Formula One:	From 1999
Grands Prix contested:	16
Wins:	None
Pole positions:	None
Fastest laps:	None

Drivers and Results 1999

Driver	Nationality	Races	Wins	Pts	Pos
Mika Salo	Finnish	3	0	0	N/A
Jacques Villeneuve	Canadian	16	0	0	N/A
Ricardo Zonta	Brazilian	13	0	0	N/A

Car specifications

Sponsors:	British American Tobacco, Teleglobe
Team principal:	Craig Pollock
Team manager:	Robert Synge
Designer:	Malcolm Oastler
Chief engineer:	Jock Clear
Test driver:	Darren Manning
Chassis:	BAR 02
Engine:	Honda V10

BETTER LUCK IN 2000?: BAR designer Malcolm Oastler will be hoping that his second Formula One chassis proves more successful than his first did last season

JACQUES VILLENEUVE

STILL A CHARGER

Jacques Villeneuve teamed up last year with his mentor Craig Pollock's all-new BAR team and he came away with nothing. This year there must be some top results to keep one of Formula One's true chargers happy.

Jacques Villeneuve came close to winning on his Grand Prix debut in 1996 and since then has gathered points almost at will. Even as Williams fell into decline in 1998. So last season must have come as such a shock, as his record read 16 starts, four finishes and not even a single point.

Noone said life at British American Racing was going to be easy, but it was never imagined that it would prove this difficult. Initial boasts that the team would win on its debut were downplayed and proved wide of the mark. But the team run by Jacques' friend and former manager Craig Pollock still expected to win at least a race or two.

Yet, Jacques never stopped attacking. There were flashes of promise such as qualifying fifth at Imola and running third at Barcelona. But it was an achievement if he qualified in the top ten. As for scoring points, Jacques didn't see the finish line until the Belgian Grand Prix. Ironically, this was after he and team-mate Ricardo Zonta destroyed their cars against the barriers at Eau Rouge in practice.

Jacques kept positive, save for an outburst against Pollock's co-founder Adrian Reynard mid-season, and earned great respect for never giving less than 100 per cent. In truth, he doesn't know any other way, much like his late father. BAR has works Honda engines for the season ahead. And, if these can be united with an improved chassis and infinitely improved reliability, Jacques will do the rest.

A double champion

Jacques is the son of the late Gilles Villeneuve. And although he spent his childhood following the Grand Prix circus, it came as a surprise when he turned to racing in the late 1980s. After three years in Italian Formula Three, he met up with Pollock when he raced to second overall in Japanese Formula Three in 1992. And Pollock helped sort Jacques a drive in Toyota Atlantic. He landed an Indycar ride for 1994, finishing as top rookie. In 1995, he not only won the Indy 500 but also three other races to scoop the title.

Bernie Ecclestone helped Jacques into a ride with Williams for 1996. With Williams dominating, Jacques won five races and pushed team-mate Damon Hill for the title.

HANGING LOOSE: Jacques Villeneuve's boots weren't the only things that came undone in 1999

TRACK NOTES

Nationality: . . . . .CANADIAN
Born: . . . . .APRIL 9, 1971,
    ST JEAN-SUR-RICHELIEU, CANADA
Teams: . . . . . .WILLIAMS 1996–1998,
    . . . . .BAR 1999–2000

Career record
First Grand Prix: 1996 AUSTRALIAN GP
Grand Prix starts: 65
Grand Prix wins: 11
    *(1996 European GP, 1996 British GP,
    1996 Hungarian GP, 1996 Portuguese
    GP, 1997 Brazilian GP, 1997
    Argentinian GP, 1997 Spanish GP, 1997
    British GP, 1997 Hungarian GP, 1997
    Austrian GP, 1997 Luxembourg GP)*
Poles: .13
Fastest laps: 9
Points: 180
Honours: . . .1997 WORLD CHAMPION,
    1996 FORMULA ONE RUNNER-UP,
    1995 INDYCAR CHAMPION, 1994
    INDYCAR ROOKIE OF THE YEAR, 1993
    TOYOTA ATLANTIC ROOKIE OF THE
    YEAR, 1992 JAPANESE FORMULA
    THREE RUNNER-UP

Jacques became the team's number one for 1998 and won seven times to go to the final round at Jerez with only Michael Schumacher standing between himself and the title. Famously, they clashed but Jacques survived to become World Champion.

The 1998 season was a struggle as Williams fell behind the McLarens and Ferraris with a car that was a handful, with Jacques driving well to collect two thirds, making his departure for BAR all the easier.

RICARDO ZONTA

IN NEED OF RESULTS

Ricardo Zonta was expected to impress in 1999, but BAR failed to offer him a car that was either competitive or reliable. And this quick Brazilian needs one in 2000 so he can attempt to match team-mate Jacques Villeneuve.

Nationality: . . . . .BRAZILIAN
Born: . . . . .MARCH 23, 1976,
. . . . .CURITIBA, BRAZIL
Teams: . . . . .BAR 1999–2000

Career record

First Grand Prix: 1999 AUSTRALIAN GP
Starts: 12
Wins: . . . . .NONE
Pole positions: . . . . .NONE
Fastest laps: . . . . .NONE
Points: . . . . .NONE
Honours: . . .1998 FIA GT CHAMPION,
1997 FORMULA 3000 CHAMPION, 1995
SOUTH AMERICAN AND BRAZILIAN
FORMULA THREE CHAMPION

A FURROWED BROW: Ricardo Zonta found few reasons to smile in his injury-interrupted first season

Ricardo has retained his place at BAR for a second year in which the team must come up with the equipment with which Ricardo must score some more concrete results.

A regular winner

Ricardo came to Formula One armed with a host of titles as he had cut a swathe through the junior formulae. He won both the Brazilian and South American Formula Three championships in 1995 before coming to Europe to race in Formula 3000. His first season with the Draco team saw him come good at season's end to win twice and rank fourth overall. Changing across to the crack Super Nova team for 1997, he duly raced to three wins and the title by a small margin over Juan Pablo Montoya.

McLaren then signed him up on a management deal and Mercedes placed Ricardo with its sportscar team. Ricardo then did everything expected of him and more by winning five rounds to clinch the FIA GT Championship. Then British American Tobacco team wanted a South American driver in one of the seats at BAR and Ricardo fitted the bill.

The one thing that Ricardo Zonta needed in his first season of Formula One was a reliable car with which to gain valuable racing mileage. And, with British American Racing suffering from diabolical reliability in its first season, that's one thing that he didn't have.

On top of this, Ricardo required – as all Formula One newcomers do – a team that offered him support. And, with BAR suffering all sorts of internal struggles, that was something else that he lacked.

Add to this the fact that he had a huge accident practising for his home Grand Prix at Interlagos and damaged the tendons in his left foot to such an extent that he missed this race

and the next three, and it's scarcely surprising that the once-smiling Brazilian completed his first season with people enquiring whether this really was the hotshot that he'd been made out to be.

Being number two driver in a team that's not making much headway in looking after its number one is no place to do a great deal, but despite outpacing team-mate Jacques Villeneuve in their sketchy and frequently interrupted pre-season tests, Ricardo outqualified the Canadian only in the lottery of the wet session at Magny-Cours. And he fared no better in the races, indeed finishing only four times, with eighth place in the European Grand Prix at the Nurburgring his best.

MINARDI

LOOKING EVER BETTER

Never blessed with much of a budget or with experienced drivers, Minardi looks in fair shape this season, with what's expected to be a good chassis powered by a Ford engine. So, points may become less of a miracle.

There were moments of great excitement for Minardi last year when it was involved in protracted negotiations with Marc Gene's sponsor, Telefonica. The Spanish telecommunications company wanted to invest in the team, to give it the financial footing that it had craved for so long. The financial footing that would allow it to develop its car and propel it up into the midfield.

However, these negotiations also brought a hint of sadness, as suggestions were made that Telefonica would want to relocate the team to Spain, to take this most Italian team away from its Italian of roots.

At the time of writing, one Spanish element is definitely in place for 2000: Marc Gene. He signed up at the eleventh hour last year and had even the sport's insiders rushing around trying to discover where he'd come from. It was from Formula Open Fortuna, a new Spanish single-seater formula that he'd won after dropping out of Formula 3000 due to a lack of finance. Part of his prize had been a test with Minardi at which he'd impressed. He then found some money and the rest is history. Before the year was out, Marc had confounded his critics and scored a point, which is something never to be sniffed at for a Minardi driver.

EX-FERRARI MAN: Gustav Brunner reminisces what it was like to have his cars at the front of the grid

FOR THE RECORD

Country of origin:	....................................Italy
Team base:	........................Faenza, Italy
Date of formation:	1980
Active years in Formula One:	...............From 1985
Grands Prix contested:	237
Wins:	......................................None
Pole positions:	.................................None
Fastest laps:	...................................None

Drivers and Results 1999

Driver	Nationality	Races	Wins	Pts	Pos
Luca Badoer	Italian	15	0	0	N/A
Marc Gene	Spanish	16	0	1	17th
Stephane Sarrazin	French	1	0	0	N/A

Car specifications

Sponsors:	...........Telefonica, Fondmetal, Roces, DOIMO
Team principals:	.........Giancarlo Minardi & Gabriele Rumi
Team manager:	.........................Cesare Fiorio
Designer:	.............................Gustav Brunner
Chief engineer:	.........................Gabriele Tredozi
Test driver:	....................................tba
Chassis:	..............................Minardi M02
Engine:	...............................Supertec V10

THE MONEY MAN: Gabriele Rumi has invested a fortune in Minardi, but still more money is required to move the team forward from the back of the grid

On the chassis front, Gustav Brunner is expected to design another tidy and effective chassis. And if it makes as much progress through the season as last year's did, then Minardi will stand a good chance of adding to their points tally. However, what ought to help more is the arrival of ex-works Ford engines in place of the customer Ford engines used in 1999. This means, at least, that Minardi will be able to have more of a crack at joining the midfield. But fellow 1999 strugglers Arrows have also upgraded, to Supertec engines, as they both try to power their way off the back of the grid.

Sponsor Telefonica chose the team's second driver as it wanted a South American, preferably a Spanish speaker.

A tougher approach

For years, to understand Giancarlo Minardi the man was to understand Minardi the team. He goes racing for the pleasure, to be involved. Loved by everyone in the paddock for his indomitable attitude and his sheer delight at the occasional point coming the team's way, Giancarlo would always be back for more, trying to get by on not much of a budget, ever looking for David to put one over Goliath. However, since the arrival of co-owner Gabriele Rumi, the team has been trying to lay to rest the image of being the eternal underdog. Rumi, of course, arrived not only with wealth from his Fondmetal alloy wheels business, but also with Formula One experience from running his own team between 1990 and 1992. Indeed,

Rumi now owns a larger share of the team than its founder. And it is he who has been responsible for the arrival of personnel such as former Ferrari team boss Cesare Fiorio as sporting director and Gustav Brunner as technical director.

Ever the optimists

A look back over Minardi's history reveals that the team's drivers have scored only 28 points since the team broke into Formula One in 1985. However, as ever, they hope to change all that...

Pierluigi Martini was the first to drive for the team when it had a one-car effort in 1985. He left, but returned in 1988 and scored Minardi's first point. The following year produced the team's finest moment when Martini led the Portuguese Grand Prix for a lap. He then opened his 1990 campaign by qualifying on the front row at Phoenix, but amazingly failed to score all year. A pair of fourth places were his reward in 1991, when the team used the previous year's Ferrari engines. These were the team's best ever results, in a year that saw the team record its best ever finish in the Constructors' Cup: seventh overall. A third fourth place was recorded by Christian Fittipaldi in the 1993 South African Grand Prix. Then a fourth fourth place looked to be in the bag for Luca Badoer at last year's European Grand Prix, but his gearbox failed. At least the team came away with a point that day as Gene kept Eddie Irvine's Ferrari at bay in the closing laps for sixth place...

MARC GENE

A SURPRISING TALENT

Many Formula One insiders hadn't even heard of Marc Gene before he grabbed the second Minardi ride last year. However, the Spaniard kept on learning through 1999, came away with a point and should go better still in 2000.

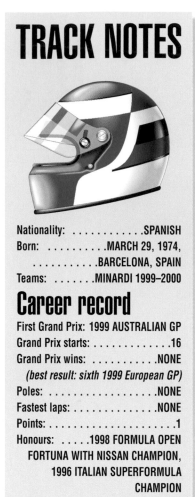

SOPHOMORE PRESSURE: Marc Gene knows that Formula One becomes serious in a driver's second year

Noone has ever been more delighted at scoring a World Championship point than Marc Gene was when he drove his Minardi across the finish line in sixth place at last year's European Grand Prix at the Nurburgring. Certainly, it had been an extraordinary wet/dry race, but he had found himself ahead of championship leaders Mika Hakkinen and Eddie Irvine with just a few laps to go and lost a place only to the Finn. Exasperated and amused, he had made his mark and given Minardi the point that earned the team its crucial travel money for 2000.

However, that wasn't the Spaniard's only highlight in 1999. Indeed, there were plenty. Drafted into the team at the last minute when Esteban Tuero decided not to stay on, he went well in a test at Barcelona before the cars departed for Australia. Some said that this was because the test had been at his home circuit, but knowledge is one thing, going out and doing it is another.

As with any driver in Formula One, Marc's benchmark was his team-mate, Luca Badoer. And Marc did well, outqualifying the experienced Italian six times. However, as the team developed its chassis, there were occasions when Marc flew, with the German Grand Prix an example when he broke clear of the back two rows of the grid to qualify fifteenth ahead of drivers of some considerably more powerful cars.

With his sixth place backed up by an eighth and four ninth places, Marc has shown an ability to bring his car home. Whether or not that enables him to move to a midfield team remains to be seen, but this likeable Spaniard is a welcome addition to Formula One.

Trained in Britain
Marc combined a university course in England with a year in the British Formula Ford series in 1993. Moving up to Formula Three in 1994, the Mitsubishi engine he used that year wasn't the one to have. His second season of British Formula Three produced one third place and little more, so a season in Italian Superformula followed and he won the title. Marc's career appeared to be running out of steam when he dropped out of Formula 3000 midway through 1997 due to a lack of funds. Then, as if by a stroke of luck, a new racing series was invented in Spain for 1998. This was called Formula Open Fortuna by Nissan and was much like Formula 3000. Marc took to it like a duck to water and raced to six straight wins and the title, the prize for which was a test drive with Minardi. The rest is history.

NORBERTO FONTANA

SECOND TIME AROUND

Argentina longs for a Formula One star of its own, a latter-day Carlos Reutemann if you like. Norberto Fontana failed at his first attempt with Sauber in 1997 but is now back from the wilderness with Minardi to try again.

TRACK NOTES

Nationality: . . . . .ARGENTINIAN
Born: . . . . .20 JANUARY 1975,
. . . . .ARREATES, ARGENTINA
Teams: .SAUBER 1997, MINARDI 2000

Career record
First Grand Prix: . . .1997 FRENCH GP
Grand Prix starts: 4
Grand Prix wins: . . . . .NONE
(best result: ninth, 1997 British GP, 1997 German GP)
Poles: . . . . .NONE
Fastest laps: . . . . .NONE
Points: . . . . .NONE
Honours: . .1995 GERMAN FORMULA THREE CHAMPION
HOTTEST DRIVE: WINNING 1995 MARLBORO MASTERS FORMULA THREE RACE AT ZANDVOORT
BIGGEST SETBACK: LOSING 1996 FORMULA NIPPON TITLE TO RALF SCHUMACHER

Few countries have a Formula One history as proud as Argentina's. In the 1950s, Argentinian drivers shone, and none did so as brightly as Juan Manuel Fangio who raced to a record five Formula One titles. The country's best driver since has been Reutemann who starred in the 1970s. Their Grand Prix has come and gone since then, but a top-line driver has yet to leave their shores.

Think back to 1998 and the Minardi team ran another Argentinian, Esteban Tuero. But he was a driver of no notable pedigree and retreated after one year to lick his wounds in national touring car races at home. Norberto, too, has tried Formula One without success, but he's back for more thanks to Minardi sponsor Telefonica wanting a Spanish-speaking South American in the team's second seat.

Norberto set sail for Europe at the start of 1993 at the age of 18, albeit looking much younger. He immediately started beating more experienced drivers in Formula Ford, so he and his healthy budget were welcomed to the KMS team for an attack on the 1994 German Formula Three title. Three wins followed and Norberto placed sixth overall.

This was followed by his elevation to test driver for Sauber and a second campaign in German Formula Three. Norberto raced to four wins in the first four races, then won a further six en route to the title, with Ralf Schumacher a distant runner-up. He also beat Schumacher to win the Marlboro Masters international invitation race at Zandvoort, sending his reputation through the roof.

Rising in the east
Fate would have it that Ralf Schumacher followed Norberto to Formula Nippon for 1996. But the tables were turned as the German landed the championship at the final round, with Norberto ending up fifth overall despite winning a round. A one-off Formula 3000 race at Estoril was added to his programme so that he could learn the track before a test with Sauber, but he was almost tipped over in a collision in the race.

The test with Sauber failed to land him the drive he craved for 1997. Fate played its hand, though, and Norberto was drafted into the Swiss team at the French GP when Gianni Morbidelli was injured. His drive was marred by a lack of testing. However, his next two outings produced a pair of ninths, but he was more than a second off team-mate Johnny Herbert's lap times. In Formula Nippon, he again won once to rank third as Pedro de la Rosa dominated. With no Formula One opening for 1998, Norberto stayed for a third year in Formula Nippon, again winning once, and ranked fourth.

Norberto raced in Formula 3000 in 1999, but despite his best results being a pair of fifths, then came the call from Telefonica...

A SECOND CHANCE: Norberto Fontana received a last-minute reprieve

DRIVERS TO WATCH

We all know who this year's Formula One drivers are. But it's worth taking a look at those bubbling under, as they're the stars of the future.

It was much simpler back in the 1950s and 1960s when there were two ways that a driver could make it to Formula One: either by ability or by the opening of the family coffers. It's not like that any more, as almost no families have coffers large enough to finance such an extravagance. Furthermore, there are fewer drives to go for, with no occasional seats being up for hire for each Grand Prix. Nowadays there are still two routes into Formula One and they are very different routes. One is direct and according to talent, the other is via the test teams. Each Formula One team has one now and it's a way for a driver to get his foot in the door. It works too – just ask Damon Hill who chose this route when his endeavours in Formula 3000 hadn't proved enough for any team to offer him a ride. So he signed up to be test driver for Williams, doing the 'dirty work' in support of the team's race drivers Nigel Mansell and Riccardo Patrese. This not only offered Damon the opportunity to gain useful mileage in a Formula One car, but also offered the team a direct comparison of his speed and skills against those of its race drivers, rather than guessing about a driver's real skill level when watching him compete in the junior formulae. Damon's gamble paid off and he landed a ride with the race team for the following season, even scoring his first Grand

LEARNING STATESIDE: Juan Pablo Montoya should carry on winning in the USA before rejoining Williams

Prix win before the season was out. Damon had chosen well, then, as he'd not just landed a Formula One drive, but a drive with the top team of the time, something that might have taken him year after year to land had he simply entered Formula One with a race ride with one of the tail-end teams.

David Coulthard echoed this route in from the Williams test team to the race team in 1994, with his elevation due to Ayrton Senna's death at Imola. Formula One test drivers can even be sub-divided into those who do the job full-time, having failed to earn promotion to a Formula One race team through their efforts in its feeder category Formula 3000, and those who land a testing deal alongside their Formula 3000 race programmes. The latter group are largely the men on a fast track to Formula One. And among their rank for 2000 is Bruno Junqueira who is tipped as Formula 3000 title favourite as well as landing a testing deal with Williams through backing from the British team's fuel supplier, Petrobras.

Likewise, Enrique Bernoldi is expected to be test driver for Sauber and Luciano Burti for Jaguar Racing. They're all quick and they're all Brazilian. Frenchman Stephane Sarrazin is likely to dice for the Formula 3000 title with them as well as possibly being test driver for Prost again. Another French driver, Nicolas Minassian, is also worth watching out for, as he was one of only six winners in Formula 3000 last year.

Formula 3000 is a trying scene, with more than 40 drivers going out onto the track at the same time last year in an attempt to qualify. And to think that Formula One drivers complain of traffic... However, several drivers tipped for success had rotten seasons, with Briton Oliver Gavin ending up with a team that didn't appear to deliver either for him or for team-mate Jamie Davies. Likewise, Frenchman Soheil Ayari had a disappointing time. Northern Ireland's Kevin McGarrity started his year with a second place at Imola, but his year went backwards from there. The best British rookie in Formula 3000 was the promising Justin Wilson who was in the points in his first race and is sure to score more points in the season ahead.

Japan has Formula Nippon, which is its version of Formula 3000, and the honours were split between Dutchman Tom Coronel and local aces Satoshi Motoyama and Hideshi Mitsusada.

You should also put the names of all the national Formula Three champions in your notebook. They are British champion Marc Hynes, French champion Sebastien Bourdais,

German champion Christijan Albers, Japanese champion Darren Manning (he's British) and South American champion Hoover Orsi. The Italian Formula Three Championship has seen all the top Italian drivers bar Jarno Trulli pass through it, but it's in decline and the Swedish driver who won last year's Italian title, Peter Sundberg, isn't expected to go shooting to the top. Italy has good reason to worry about the level of its representation at the top in the years to come, as its brightest stars have not even raced at Formula Three level yet. Keep your eyes peeled, though, for last year's European Formula Renault champion Gianmaria Bruni, a driver who clinched the title at the final round ahead of a Brazilian driver by the name of Antonio Pizzonia who stormed the British Formula Renault series and has set himself the target of being a Formula One driver within three years.

Compared to the Italians, British racing fans have much more reason to celebrate, with Jenson Button seen very much as a future champion. He started in car racing in 1998 after a stunning childhood in karting, winning the Formula Ford title at his first attempt. His graduation to Formula Three saw Jenson qualify

FLYING SCOT: Dario Franchitti was equal on points with Montoya in '99, but also wants a Formula One ride

on pole for his first race and win his third. He ended the year as runner-up but has eshewed a move to Formula 3000 and is staying on for a further year in Formula Three so that he can win the title. Whether he does or not, this 19-year-old has extremely good support and is expected to go all the way.

It's not just youth that is worth watching or employing, though, as two of the Formula One teams are opting for the experience of former Formula One drivers in their test teams, with Ferrari using Luca Badoer and McLaren using Olivier Panis after their standing down from the race teams at Minardi and Prost respectively. This may serve them well, offering more experience to make their analysis more accurate, but it does deny an up-and-coming driver of the opportunity. And this seems particularly surprising from a team such as McLaren that is respected throughout the sport for the way in which it nurtures young talent. However, it has two of its former test drivers on long-term contracts that dictate that McLaren can take up the services in the future for their race team, having farmed them out to gain Formula One race experience with midfield teams, with Ricardo Zonta racing for British American Racing and Nick Heidfeld having just joined Prost. The reason for this is that McLaren boss Ron Dennis doesn't want to entrust his precious race seats to a driver who is going to spend his first Grand Prix season making the mistakes of a novice. Better to have them ironed out first.

With just 11 teams in Formula One at present – and thus just 22 drives available – there are very few openings for drivers to land a ride. Indeed, reigning Formula 3000 driver Heidfeld is the only one making the step up. He comes armed with two years of supremely useful testing experience with McLaren. Sadly, the two drivers who finished immediately behind the German in Formula 3000 last year will never grace a Formula One seat, as Jason Watt was paralysed from the chest down after a motorcycle accident and just a month earlier his good friend and rival Gonzalo Rodriguez was killed contesting a Champ Car race.

Talking of the largely North American Champ Car series, the two drivers who scored the most points in it last year both have their eyes on a Formula One ride in the future. They are Colombian Juan Pablo Montoya and Scotland's Dario Franchitti.

Traditionally, the route through Champ Cars hasn't been a much used passage to Formula

TIPPED FOR THE TOP: Bruno Junqueira is Williams' test driver and Formula 3000 title favourite

One, with only Michael Andretti in 1993, Jacques Villeneuve in 1996 and Alessandro Zanardi in 1999 heading back across the pond. Indeed, Zanardi had already raced for several years in Formula One before heading west. However, the less than sparkling form of Andretti and Zanardi has not been a good example for Champ Cars. Villeneuve was a different case, though, coming close to winning the world title in his first year with Williams. And this showed the benefit to be had from making the jump into a top team and also of having a winter of testing.

Montoya has already spent a year as test driver for Williams, in the same year as winning the Formula 3000 title two seasons ago. Williams has him on a long-term contract. Indeed, with people expressing disappointment at Zanardi failing to score a point for the team last year, there was talk of bringing Montoya back to Williams a year ahead of schedule. But he plans to honour his contract with his Champ Car team boss Chip Ganassi.

Franchitti, on the other hand, has ties with Jaguar Racing, formerly Stewart, having spent his formative years with the team's junior arm: Paul Stewart Racing. He certainly wouldn't be averse to coming back across and taking up a ride as number two to Eddie Irvine at the team in green in 2001.

As to the young talent that is beneath this duo in Champ Cars, sadly Greg Moore crashed to his death at last year's final round. However, Brazilian drivers Helio Castro Neves and Tony Kanaan are seen as ones to watch, but the majority of winning is done, Franchitti and Montoya apart, by drivers who are happily settled into Champ Car racing and unlikely to make the crossover to Formula One. And, as for Indy Lights, Champ Cars' feeder formula, that doesn't appear to be blessed with any exceptional talent right now, although Northern Ireland's Johnny Kane became a race winner at last year's final round. Judging by his skill on oval race tracks, though, expect Johnny to be looking more to Champ Cars for his future.

So, there are a host of championships to look out for, but every hotshot knows that no matter how good they are, they have to have more than talent and financial backing. Like a surfer, they have to catch the right wave and to be the one with momentum when an opportunity opens up, whether for a race seat or a berth in the test team.

**FRANCE EXPECTS: Stephane
Sarrazin shone on his brief Formula
One debut and is anxious for more**

F1 LIFE IN THE OTHER FAST LANE

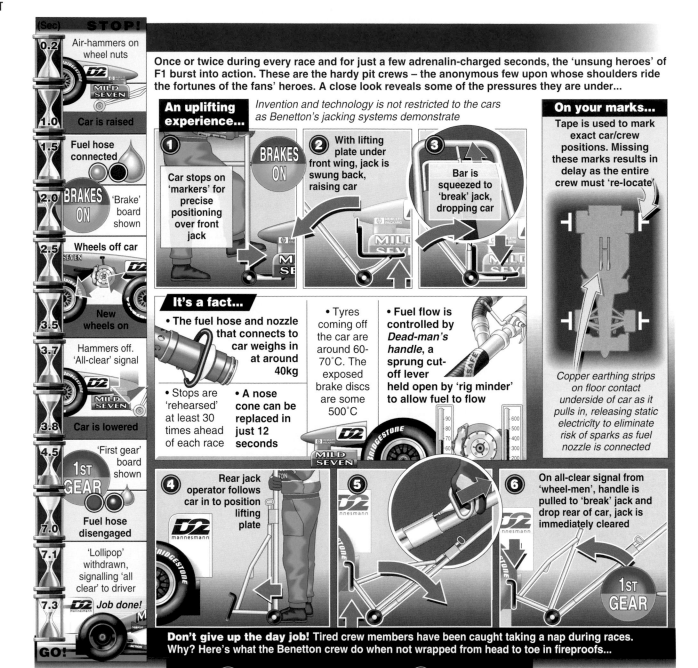

Once or twice during every race and for just a few adrenalin-charged seconds, the 'unsung heroes' of F1 burst into action. These are the hardy pit crews – the anonymous few upon whose shoulders ride the fortunes of the fans' heroes. A close look reveals some of the pressures they are under...

(Sec) STOP!

Time	Event
0.2	Air-hammers on wheel nuts
1.0	Car is raised
1.5	Fuel hose connected
2.0	BRAKES ON – 'Brake' board shown
2.5	Wheels off car
3.5	New wheels on
3.7	Hammers off. 'All-clear' signal
3.8	Car is lowered
4.5	'First gear' board shown – 1ST GEAR
7.0	Fuel hose disengaged
7.1	'Lollipop' withdrawn, signalling 'all clear' to driver
7.3	Job done!

GO!

An uplifting experience...

Invention and technology is not restricted to the cars as Benetton's jacking systems demonstrate

1 Car stops on 'markers' for precise positioning over front jack — BRAKES ON

2 With lifting plate under front wing, jack is swung back, raising car

3 Bar is squeezed to 'break' jack, dropping car

It's a fact...

- The fuel hose and nozzle that connects to car weighs in at around 40kg
- Stops are 'rehearsed' at least 30 times ahead of each race
- A nose cone can be replaced in just 12 seconds
- Tyres coming off the car are around 60-70°C. The exposed brake discs are some 500°C
- Fuel flow is controlled by *Dead-man's handle*, a sprung cut-off lever held open by 'rig minder' to allow fuel to flow

On your marks...

Tape is used to mark exact car/crew positions. Missing these marks results in delay as the entire crew must 're-locate'

Copper earthing strips on floor contact underside of car as it pulls in, releasing static electricity to eliminate risk of sparks as fuel nozzle is connected

4 Rear jack operator follows car in to position lifting plate

5

6 On all-clear signal from 'wheel-men', handle is pulled to 'break' jack and drop rear of car, jack is immediately cleared — 1ST GEAR

Don't give up the day job! Tired crew members have been caught taking a nap during races. Why? Here's what the Benetton crew do when not wrapped from head to toe in fireproofs...

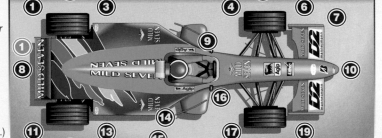

1: Wheel OFF (Gearbox) – after removing wheel, takes up position at rear of car, to stand-by with starter

2: Hammer (Mechanic)

3: Wheel ON (Mechanic)

4: Wheel ON (Mechanic)

5: Hammer (Fabricator)

6: Wheel OFF (Mechanic)

7: Brake board (Chief Mech.)

8: Rear jack (Truckie)

9: Car balance (Engine)

10: Front jack (Mechanic)

11: Wheel ON (Mechanic)

12: Hammer (Mechanic)

13: Wheel OFF (Hydraulics)

14: Refueller (Truckie)

15: Hose support (Truckie)

16: Visor wipe (Electronics)

17: Wheel ON (Mechanic)

18: Hammer (Fabricator)

19: Wheel OFF (Mechanic)

Graphic: © Russell Lewis

A FINE WAY TO START A RACE

The complete race start sequencing begins 30 minutes before the formation lap is scheduled to begin, when the cars will leave the pits to take up their grid positions. Fifteen minutes later the main red lights come on and any car still in the pits must wait until the last car has passed the pit exit, following the race start, before being allowed to get under way.

The adrenalin really starts pumping, however, as the five-minute signal is given and the final countdown begins...

5:00
First pair of red lights extinguished

3:00
Everyone except team members and race officials leave grid

1:00
Engines started
All remaining personnel must leave grid

0:30
Single set of red lights remain illuminated

0:00
Green lights signal start of **formation lap**

Aborted formation lap
Orange lights flash until new start time is confirmed – normally 15 minutes later

Mirror, mirror... They may look too small to be of much use, but in the critical opening stages of a Grand Prix, a driver's mirrors are a major asset!

-0:05

MILD SEVEN
BRIDGESTONE   BRIDGESTONE

-0:04
-0:03
-0:02
-0:01

On the green light...
The single formation lap is more important than may be immediately obvious.

Drivers must take this last opportunity to look for any changes in track surface or conditions, while at the same time trying to get as much heat as possible into tyres and

Wait for it... when all 22 cars have come to a halt in their starting positions, the countdown begins.
Five seconds to go...
The critical moment, as the first set of red lights is illuminated. Absolute concentration must now remain balanced between watching the lighting sequence and maintaining optimum engine revs

One second to go...
All five sets of red lights are on. With engines screaming all around them, drivers must focus 100%, waiting for 'lights out'

0:00

GO, GO, GO!...
Last red lights go out after pre-set delay (3 seconds), and the charge for the first corner is on. As cars accelerate to 100mph in around three seconds, a split-second can make or break a weekend's work...

Five big steps to 'Turn 1'

When the lights go out, 'all-round' concentration becomes the key

1: The first priority is to get away cleanly, controlling wheel-spin and getting the power down smoothly

2: Look for the car ahead and go for any 'gaps' in the field – checking both left and right

3: Driver must be alert to all of the cars around him, defending his own position to avoid losing any places

4: 'Claim' position and steady the car

5: Now driver must look for 'turn one' and find enough road for a clean run through

But what if?...

If race start is aborted after formation lap:
Orange lights flash. If five second countdown has begun, lights freeze in current state. All main lights go out when re-start time is confirmed – delay normally five minutes.
Countdown resumes at three minutes as normal start procedure (three sets of red lights)

If the race is stopped...

1: All red lights come on, pit lane remains open.
2: When re-start time is confirmed all red lights go out.
3: Ten minutes after red flag is shown, pit lane is closed. Main red lights come on, flashing twice. Three minutes before new parade lap, two pairs of red lights go out, horn sounds and normal start procedure is resumed

Art. 138:
Up to 12-litres of fuel may be added on grid, *prior to* 5-minute signal

Art. 139:
All wheels must be fitted by the time 5-minute signal is shown

Art. 148: Jump starts will be punished by 10-second penalty

GRAPHIC: © Russell Lewis

Start variations: *Track is dry throughout practice sessions, but becomes wet after warm-up (or vice-versa):* a 15-minute free practice may be allowed.
Rain begins to fall after 'five-minute' signal:
Race Director may allow teams to change tyres. In this case, abort lights show, countdown resumes from 15-minute stage.
'Too much' water on track to start race: 'ten boards' and abort lights shown (this process can be repeated several times)

 Indicates 10 minutes to green light

 Indicates a 10-minute delay

Drive safely: If race is to be started behind safety car: yellow flashing lights will come on before the one-minute signal.

SC

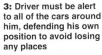

When green grid lights come on, cars move off behind safety car – *there is no formation lap.* Drivers must remain within five car lengths of each other. Any driver stationary when all other cars have crossed line, may join behind other cars – *overtaking is forbidden*

Cars may pass the safety car only if signalled to do so by 'green light'

THE F1 WHEEL OF FORTUNE...

Since the 'paddle' gear-shift mechanism first appeared on the steering wheel of a sceptical Nigel Mansell's Ferrari in Brazil, 1989, an inestimable amount of time and money has been invested in turning one of the car's most basic components into a major nerve-centre. Today's drivers have both hands firmly fixed to a technological masterpiece that is worth rather more than its weight in gold!

Function mode (–): works in conjuction with main function selector switch, button scrolls **down** through setting options. '(+)' button scrolls **up**

So what are all those flashing lights and buttons about? Read on as all is revealed...

Traffic signals: lights set in top of steering wheel give a constant guide to car's running status

'SL' (Gear shift): sequential lights pre-set to specific 'rev' bands – determined by individual circuit characteristics and conditions – tell drivers when to change gear	**A/D:** Spare
	B/C: Pit lane speed limiter on
	E: Radio indicator
	F/H: Clutch (separate left and right paddle indicators)
	G: Throttle. Pre-sets allow indication of optimum throttle level for start
	J: Second pit limiter indicator

Reverse gear: on the back of the steering wheel...

1: Gear up-shift
2: Gear down-shift
3/4: Clutch paddles

The right connections: wheel 'plugs in' to the car via a set of pins that lock into corresponding sockets on the tip of the steering column

Function mode (+)

'Flag' lights (experimental)

Spare

5

PO
P1 IGN
P2

6

SCROLL

7

Radio button

Neutral selector

Pit lane limiter button

REVERSE

Two-way engine map group switch: allows instant switching of engine maps while car is in the pits

OFF **8**
LIGHT
ON

FIRE

9

E48   16000   266
6   1:26:32   86°

Main function selector

Fuel mix : five-way switch allows fuel mixture to be modified on-track

Logger switch: Should a problem occur on-track, button can 'mark' telemetry read-out for later analysis by engineers

Screen display: a massive range of data can be displayed on integral screen. Below: a 'typical' display

Error ID: if a fault develops on-track, driver can radio code number to engineers to indentify problem

Main function switch: determines which data is displayed on screen and activates selected programme

DISP: scrolls display of pressure data on various circuits such as compressed air and brakes

FAIL: simulates selected component failure – used for testing only!

BAL: sets front-to-rear brake balance (15 settings)

Engine data and settings

THR: controls throttle function to Mecachrome specifications (5 settings)

BRK: controls engine braking effect to preserve rear brakes (5 settings)

RS: spare channel for Mechachrome settings

Reserve channels

FAIL DISP THR BRK RS BAL

Engine revs   **Speed (km/h)**

Gear —

E48   16000   266
6   1:26:32   86°

— Water temp.

Lap time – *display will flash to indicate a 'best' time*

5 **'Flag' lights:** Experimental light system operates in conjunction with trackside flag signalling

6 **Ignition:** Three-way switch. P0:off; P1:standby; P2: enables ignition

7 **Scroll:** Allows scrolling of information on data screen

8 Rear light switch   **9** Fire extinguisher switch

GETTING AROUND IN F1...

Setting up a Formula 1 car is a highly complex – not to say intricate – business. So much so, in fact, that this entire volume could be dedicated to the cause! To summarise some of the key points, however, we can can look at one aspect that can also affect many other areas.

Listen to drivers' complaints about the way their cars are performing and the most frequently heard words are 'understeer' and 'oversteer' – particularly when they have just walked back from parking in the gravel!

So just what exactly are they talking about and, more importantly, what can be done to sort the problem out?

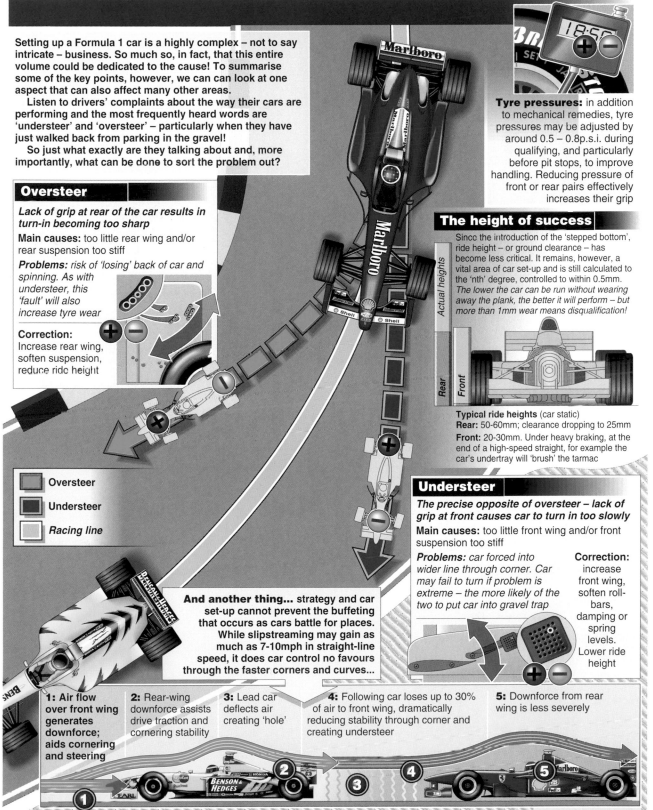

Oversteer

Lack of grip at rear of the car results in turn-in becoming too sharp

Main causes: too little rear wing and/or rear suspension too stiff

Problems: *risk of 'losing' back of car and spinning. As with understeer, this 'fault' will also increase tyre wear*

Correction: Increase rear wing, soften suspension, reduce ride height

■ Oversteer
■ Understeer
■ *Racing line*

And another thing... strategy and car set-up cannot prevent the buffeting that occurs as cars battle for places. While slipstreaming may gain as much as 7-10mph in straight-line speed, it does car control no favours through the faster corners and curves...

Tyre pressures: in addition to mechanical remedies, tyre pressures may be adjusted by around 0.5 – 0.8p.s.i. during qualifying, and particularly before pit stops, to improve handling. Reducing pressure of front or rear pairs effectively increases their grip

The height of success

Since the introduction of the 'stepped bottom', ride height – or ground clearance – has become less critical. It remains, however, a vital area of car set-up and is still calculated to the 'nth' degree, controlled to within 0.5mm. *The lower the car can be run without wearing away the plank, the better it will perform – but more than 1mm wear means disqualification!*

Actual heights

Rear *Front*

Typical ride heights (car static)
Rear: 50-60mm; clearance dropping to 25mm
Front: 20-30mm. Under heavy braking, at the end of a high-speed straight, for example the car's undertray will 'brush' the tarmac

Understeer

The precise opposite of oversteer – lack of grip at front causes car to turn in too slowly

Main causes: too little front wing and/or front suspension too stiff

Problems: *car forced into wider line through corner. Car may fail to turn if problem is extreme – the more likely of the two to put car into gravel trap*

Correction: increase front wing, soften roll-bars, damping or spring levels. Lower ride height

1: Air flow over front wing generates downforce; aids cornering and steering

2: Rear-wing downforce assists drive traction and cornering stability

3: Lead car deflects air creating 'hole'

4: Following car loses up to 30% of air to front wing, dramatically reducing stability through corner and creating understeer

5: Downforce from rear wing is less severely

Graphic: © Russell Lewis

F1

THE TRACKS

One of the beauties of Formula One is the sheer variety of venues visited. It's not like football in which a pitch is a pitch and the main change from venue to venue for the players is the quality of the changing rooms, and the main difference to the fans is the quality of the grandstands. Ask a Formula One driver if all Grand Prix circuits are the same and the answer will be a definite 'no'. They are all different. And thank goodness for that, as all fans will echo their approval of the fact that each Grand Prix offers a distinctive flavour and challenge of its own.

Examine the World Championship calendar for 2000 and the traditional venues such as Silverstone, Hockenheim and Monza are augmented not only by new circuits such as Malaysia's Sepang circuit that proved such a hit at the end of 1999, but also the all-new infield circuit at the Indianapolis Motor Speedway, the venue that has been chosen to put Formula One back on the map in the United States for the first time since it lost its foothold back in 1991. The Sepang circuit won the approval of all the drivers for its challenge, something that is all too rare at new circuits built over the past decade. On top of this, the spectators at Sepang are probably better catered for than spectators at any other circuit, with fabulous viewing from comfortable and modern grandstands. Indeed, the circuit's architect has made a template that ought to be used at other new venues in the future.

The Indianapolis Motor Speedway is already blessed with wonderful grandstands. Indeed, there are seats for upwards of 400,000 that are filled twice a year for the Indianapolis 500 Indycar race and the Brickyard 400 NASCAR stock car race. However, the regular 2.5-mile oval is not being used, so some of these are going to be defunct when the Formula One troops come to Indiana. Instead, temporary

MELBOURNE INTERLAGOS IMOLA SILVERSTONE BARCELO
A1-RING HOCKENHEIM HUNGARORING SPA-FRANC

A PLACE LIKE NO OTHER: City and race track combine to give Monaco that unique feel

grandstands are being built alongside the new circuit as it twists its way around the infield, with the regular grandstands only being used along part of the start/finish straight and Turn One. But the beauty of the track is that it is so wide. So, hopefully, there will be plenty of overtaking at this year's United States Grand Prix, something that will be essential if the race is to re-establish itself on the American sporting calendar.

Look through the calendar and there are some gems on it, with Melbourne already an established favourite, as much for the ambience of this sporting city as for its twisting circuit.

For those who want to experience passionate fans who make more noise than any others, start saving your cash for a visit to the Brazilian Grand Prix. The atmosphere

at this race is always one of party time, but you should have heard the roar when local hero Rubens Barrichello led for Stewart last year, giving the home crowd something to really get excited about for the first time since Ayrton Senna last raced there in 1994. Add to this the fact that the Interlagos circuit is a cracker and you have the ultimate package. Mind you, it's not bad at Imola either, where the *tifosi* turn out in force to cheer on the Ferraris in the San Marino Grand Prix. Of course, they're also out again later in the year for the Italian Grand Prix at Monza, which is a circuit that really must be visited by all racing fans, steeped as it is in a wonderful history. Monaco has a flavour of its own, and noone can fail to be moved by an evening walk around the perimeter of the track.

However, much of its appeal is the fashion show of the *beau monde* and a glance at the lives of the rich and famous on the massive yachts in the harbour.

For the full-on experience of a top track, there can be no season complete without a visit to Spa-Francorchamps. And if you remember what happened at Eau Rouge last year, you will understand that the drivers find this a serious challenge. Quite simply, it's magnificent.

Silverstone holds its own appeal, with the Becketts esses one of the most impressive vantage points of the year. Yet, if you want to see the drivers working to their maximum, book yourself a ringside seat for an in-car lap of Suzuka during qualifying, with the drivers having to be at their maximum for every inch of the 3.6-mile lap.

A NURBURGRING MONACO MONTREAL MAGNY-COURS
CHAMPS MONZA INDIANAPOLIS SUZUKA SEPANG

MELBOURNE

ROUND 1   MARCH 12, 2000

So established is Melbourne's Albert Park circuit after hosting just four Grands Prix that it feels as though it's part of the furniture. And long may it remain so, with teams, drivers and fans all given a fantastic start to their season.

Australian Grand Prix
M E L B O U R N E

Circuit length: 5.302km
Race distance: 58 laps

Albert Park

March
12th

Albert Park, Melbourne, 3.295 miles/5.302km. 58 laps. Lap record: Heinz-Harald Frentzen (Williams-Renault), 1m30.585s, 130.935mph, 1997

'99 results

1 Eddie Irvine	Ferrari
2 Heinz-Harald Frentzen	Jordan
3 Ralf Schumacher	Williams
4 Giancarlo Fisichella	Benetton
5 Rubens Barrichello	Stewart
6 Pedro de la Rosa	Arrows

A FULL HOUSE: The grandstands are packed as the McLarens prepare to shoot into a lead that wouldn't last

The 1994 showdown is one that will always be remembered for the battle between Michael Schumacher and Damon Hill not only to win the race but also the title. Coming under pressure for the lead from Hill, Schumacher's Benetton clipped one of the walls. Then, just as Hill tried to dive by, he hit the German, who was forced off. Sadly for Hill, he was also out, his Williams retiring with damaged suspension, giving the title to Schumacher.

All change for 1996

Victoria is the home of the Australian motorsport industry, so it was only right that its capital, Melbourne, should take over the Grand Prix. And so it did in 1996, as the season-opener, when Jacques Villeneuve looked set to win on his debut, something achieved previously only by Giancarlo Baghetti for Ferrari in 1961, but his Williams lost oil pressure and he let team-mate Hill through to win.

The second visit to Melbourne looked as though Villeneuve would waltz it for Williams after he had dominated qualifying. But he was taken out by Eddie Irvine at the first corner, and so David Coulthard was able to race on to McLaren's first win since Adelaide in 1993, with Heinz-Harald Frentzen crashing out of second in the closing laps. It was also a race that gave Hill a clue that his season was not going to go smoothly, as his Arrows coasted to a halt on the parade lap, meaning he didn't even take the start for the first race of his World title defence.

In 1998, Melbourne marked the start of McLaren's dominant year with Hakkinen and Coulthard leaving the opposition in their wake as they won by a lap. But, even winning by such a large margin left a bad taste in the mouths of some, as Hakkinen thought mistakenly that he had been called into the pits and thus lost the lead. Coulthard, though, stuck to a pre-race agreement that whichever of them entered the first corner first at the start would win the race, and so he slowed and let Hakkinen through with three laps to go to win. Race promoter Ron Walker hit the roof, but then he finds a reason to do so every year.

McLaren looked set to rule the roost in 1999, without resorting to team orders. But their cars pulled off and Eddie Irvine powered through to his first win for Ferrari while his team-mate Schumacher and Rubens Barrichello put on great charges through the field.

Melbourne's Albert Park circuit is all in a park, unlike Adelaide's part-downtown layout, and is more flowing as a result. The track runs clockwise around a lake, starting with an esse approached at 180mph leading into the second gear right-hander where Martin Brundle barrel-rolled in 1996. The track keeps bending right and the drivers hit fifth before a second gear chicane, then sixth and over 170mph before another esse. Into the back section, sweeping left, drivers hit 180mph as they take a pair of rights around the far end of the lake before completing the lap with a second-gear left-hander and a quicker right onto the main straight.

TAKING RACING TO THE PEOPLE: The Albert Park circuit enjoys a great location just a tram ride from downtown

It seems strange that it was not until 1985 that the Formula One World Championship visited Australia, but it's true. However, such has been the quality of almost every Grand Prix held there since then, whether at Adelaide or Melbourne, that it really is a cornerstone of the World Championship.

One of the most important reasons that this is such a great Grand Prix is the fact that no country knows its sport better than Australia and the organization is clear proof of that. With that, in come the spectators, many of them new to the sport and many who will be back again for a second taste next time around.

Racing downtown

Adelaide pulled off a coup when it beat its more high-profile rival cities of Sydney, Melbourne and Brisbane to land the first Australian Grand Prix in 1985. Small and cosy it may be, but the city embraced the event for 11 years and everyone loved the party atmosphere.

On top of that, Adelaide meant spectacular racing, such as the 1986 season-closer when Nigel Mansell crashed out in spectacular style after a blow-out, leaving Alain Prost to win the race and the title.

Three years later, there was more drama when a torrential downpour meant that the race was stopped early. However, by the time it was stopped, many drivers had already aquaplaned into the surrounding walls or into each other.

HERO OF THE TRACK

It's an indictment of Australia's promotion of its talent that 1980 World Champion Alan Jones remains their racing hero. But until one of his compatriots has a shot in Formula One, it's a position he'll retain. The son of a racing driver, Alan was raised in Melbourne before heading to Europe, making his Formula One debut in 1975 with a Hesketh. Drives with Hill, Surtees and Arrows followed, and his first win for Arrows in Austria in 1977 helped him join Williams. The wins flowed and he had 12 to his name when he retired.

INTERLAGOS

ROUND 2   MARCH 26, 2000

The crowd at Interlagos went mad last year when Rubens Barrichello led the race in his Stewart, so expect there to be a sea of red flags around the track now that Rubens has transferred to Ferrari.

Brazilian Grand Prix
I N T E R L A G O S

São Paulo

Circuit length: **4.292km**
Race distance: **72 laps**

March **26**th

Arquibancadas

Subida

Cotovêlo

Timing sectors

Laranja

Junção

Pinheirinho

Mergulho

Ferradura

Descida do Lago

Curva 1

Reta Oposta

Senna's S

Curva do Sol

'99 Pole: **Hakkinen**
Winner: **Hakkinen**

Interlagos, Sao Paulo, 2.667 miles/4.292km. 72 laps. Lap record: Jacques Villeneuve (Williams-Renault), 1m18.397s, 122.471mph, 1997

'99 results
1 Mika Hakkinen		McLaren
2 Michael Schumacher		Ferrari
3 Heinz-Harald Frentzen		Jordan
4 Ralf Schumacher		Williams
5 Eddie Irvine		Ferrari
6 Olivier Panis		Prost

If you have ever had the experience of attending a Grand Prix in Italy, either at Monza or at Imola, you will have an inkling of what passion Formula One can engender among the *tifosi*. But that's nothing next to the level of excitement that courses through the veins of the Brazilian fans who go quite mad when one of their own leads their Grand Prix, as Rubens Barrichello did last year.

The Brazilian Grand Prix is a carnival, a festival, a wild party. And it's held on one of the World Championship's best circuits, especially from the

BRAKE, TURN, ACCELERATE: The infield section is a series of rising and dipping corners, offering few passing places

TIGHT AND TWISTY: The first corner is not only a tight left followed by a tight right, but it drops away mid corner too

point of view of the spectators, with its bowl-like setting.

A rich history

To understand why Brazilians are so Formula One mad is to understand national identity, and their pride that such a poor country can take on and beat the world at something, football aside. The success of their multiple World Champions Emerson Fittipaldi, Nelson Piquet and Ayrton Senna is all the more stunning when you consider how Brazil is on the periphery of the racing heartland, thousands of miles away from the sport's axis in Europe. Yet each of these champions turned their back on privileged backgrounds in the Brazilian sun to chance their luck in the chilly and, to them, inhospitable climes. But how it paid off... And how even the ultra-poor who live in the shanty towns that spring up on every vacant plot around Sao Paolo worship them and support every Brazilian driver out there competing with the world's best.

Brazil yearned for a Grand Prix after Emerson Fittipaldi burst onto the racing scene in Europe in 1969. After hosting a non-championship race that was won by Carlos Reutemann in 1972, Interlagos became home to the Brazilian Grand Prix from 1973. Back then, Interlagos was a lengthy track, with a fast, open section around the perimeter linking to a twisting infield around a lake. The drivers loved it and the early years were kind to the locals, as Fittipaldi won in 1973 and 1974, for Lotus and then McLaren. In 1975, another Brazilian won, this time Carlos Pace being triumphant for Brabham.

Rio de Janeiro didn't want to miss out on the action, though, taking over in 1978 when it hosted the Grand Prix at its Jacarepagua circuit. It was never as popular as Interlagos, since its lay-out was more or less two straights linked by a handful of simple corners. Indeed, in its first year the locals went home unhappy as victory had gone not to one of their own but to Reutemann from neighbouring Argentina, who beat Fittipaldi to the chequered flag. After two years back at Interlagos, Jacarepagua regained the Grand Prix and held onto it until 1989 with Alain Prost winning there five times and Piquet twice before Interlagos took over again. Sadly, Interlagos was now unrecognizable, as it had been chopped to half of its original length, with many of the faster corners made less challenging or removed altogether.

While the changes didn't appeal to the purists, they proved good for the patriotic fans, as after years of disappointment on his home patch Senna finally won the Brazilian Grand Prix in 1991. Unsurprisingly, the crowd went berserk, but it's never been the same there since he died in 1994.

Michael Schumacher won in 1994 and 1995, Damon Hill did so in 1996, Jacques Villeneuve in 1997 and Mika Hakkinen in 1998 and 1999. So, it seems that whoever wins the Brazilian Grand Prix goes on to become World Champion.

A twisting ride

A lap of Interlagos starts with a dipping left-right chicane that is generally little problem, but a nightmare on the opening lap, as the drivers try to funnel through the corner without contact while doing their utmost to pass the cars ahead of them. For, don't forget, the first corner on the first lap is where much of the race's overtaking is done. Unsurprisingly, there have been some acrobatic shunts there, such as the one between Michael Andretti and Gerhard Berger in 1993.

A long, rising left-hander follows on to the long back straight which sees drivers hit 185mph before feeding into a tight left-hander, Descida do Lago. There is often overtaking down the inside here under braking before the long climb to the fifth gear Ferradura right-hander. It gets twisty from here on, starting with a second gear right-hander that tips the track down to another second gear corner, Pinheirinho then up to the even tighter Bico de Plato. But then it's down the hill and up through the gearbox before the last corner, Juncao, out of which drivers hope they can get a good tow all the way up the hill onto the pit straight and be in a position to make a move into that opening esse as the drivers haul their cars down from 190mph.

HERO OF THE TRACK

Until Rubens Barrichello wins a World Championship, or at least one Brazilian Grand Prix, the late Ayrton Senna will remain the driver in the hearts of the fans at Interlagos. Ayrton stormed the junior championships in Britain, landed a drive in Formula One with Toleman in 1984 then became a Grand Prix winner for Lotus in 1985 before becoming World Champion with McLaren in 1988, something he repeated twice before moving to Williams in 1994, when he died at Imola and pitched his nation into mourning.

IMOLA

ROUND 3   APRIL 9, 2000

Imola is one of Europe's best circuits, providing a magnificent spectacle as it twists and turns and rises and dips around its parkland setting, with the ever-enthusiastic tifosi adding to the atmosphere.

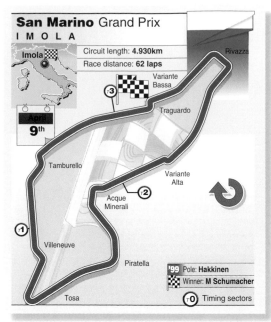

San Marino Grand Prix
I M O L A

Imola
April 9th

Circuit length: **4.930km**
Race distance: **62 laps**

Rivazza
Variante Bassa
Traguardo
Variante Alta
Acque Minerali
Tamburello
Villeneuve
Piratella
Tosa

'99 Pole: **Hakkinen**
Winner: **M Schumacher**

Timing sectors

Imola, Italy, 3.063 miles/4.930km. 62 laps. Lap record: Heinz-Harald Frentzen (Williams-Renault), 1m25.531s, 128.942mph,1997

'99 results

1 Michael Schumacher	Ferrari	
2 David Coulthard	McLaren	
3 Rubens Barrichello	Stewart	
4 Damon Hill	Jordan	
5 Giancarlo Fisichella	Benetton	
6 Jean Alesi	Sauber	

ON TOP OF THE HILL: Michael Schumacher sends the flags waving as he blasts his Ferrari out of Variante Alta

It's true that time stands still in no sport, but Formula One moves ahead with greater speed than any other. And this is why it feels as though Imola has held a Grand Prix for ever, even though it was only in 1980 that Imola first held a round of the World Championship. It was allowed the Italian Grand Prix that year, as Formula One was still wary of Monza, the longtime home of Italian racing, following Ronnie Peterson's death there two years earlier. Since then, however, Imola has hosted a Grand Prix of its own early in the season, with the Italian Grand Prix reverting to Monza in September. You may well ask why Italy is permitted to hold two Grands Prix a year while other countries have to make do with one, but that's how it is, and the race is allowed and is known as the San Marino

Grand Prix, after the nearby principality. With the Ferrari fans – the *tifosi* – out in force, both Grands Prix in Italy are a sell-out, as are all the stalls selling Ferrari memorabilia and clothing.

Hard on the cars

One factor that is always the same is that races at Imola are famous for cars not lasting the distance, as the circuit's combination of flat-out sprints and numerous areas of heavy braking takes its toll. Unfortunately, Imola is also famous for major accidents, particularly at the original Tamburello sweeper beyond the pitlane exit, as experienced by Nelson Piquet at Tamburello in 1987 and Gerhard Berger two years later.

RARE POINTS: Damon Hill finished fourth for what would prove to be the best result of his final season for Jordan

The San Marino Grand Prix has often provided some of the best racing of the year, and few drivers win there more than once. The 1997 Grand Prix was one of the best for years, with Jacques Villeneuve, Heinz-Harald Frentzen and Michael Schumacher all leading. Schumacher nosed his Ferrari ahead for only one lap during the pitstops and it was Frentzen who came good for Williams after a troubled start to his season. David Coulthard triumphed in 1998, despite a plastic bag blocking one of his radiators and sending his engine's temperature soaring which allowed Ferrari's Michael Schumacher to close in. Then in 1999 Mika Hakkinen crashed out of the lead as he powered out of Traguardo, the right-hander onto the start/finish straight, and handed the race to the chasing Michael Schumacher ahead of Coulthard who struggled in traffic and Stewart's Rubens Barrichello.

Last year marked the fifth anniversary of Ayrton Senna's death at Imola, and that of rookie Roland Ratzenberger, and it's now high time to lay that dark passage to rest and consider Imola in a more favourable light. It will take years to move out from the shadow cast over it in those two dark days in 1994, but Imola still excites as the tarmac threads along the banks of a river before twisting up and down over a wooded hilltop.

Up and down

A lap of Imola starts with a flat-out sprint past the start/finish line. This used to feed into an all-but-flat-out left-hand kink called Tamburello. But since Senna left the track there with a fatal outcome, it has been slowed by a chicane that requires the use of second gear rather than sixth... A good length straight leads down to Villeneuve, a right-hand kink where Ratzenberger hit the wall that same year. This too has been kinked and slowed, taking the sting out of the entry to Tosa corner, and at a stroke removing one of the season's best overtaking spots.

The track exits the left-hand hairpin at Tosa and climbs to Piratella, a left-hander on the crest of the wooded hilltop. From here, the track plunges down to the Acque Minerali right-hander before rising again to the Variante Alta chicane from where it drops again to the level of the start/finish straight via the double-apex Rivazza left-hander which forces drivers to slow from 185mph. The penultimate corner, Variante Bassa, has been made less extreme as a result of Rubens Barrichello's huge accident there, also in 1994. And this feeds into the left-right at Traguardo to complete the lap. Imola is not as fast as it was before the insertion of chicanes, and it's lost the best of its rhythm, but overtaking is still a possibility.

A visit to Imola makes it abundantly clear that only one team counts as far as the *tifosi* are concerned: Ferrari. Indeed, Enzo Ferrari named the circuit after his son Dino who died young. And the level of excitement emanating from a scarlet-clad, Ferrari flag-waving thousands camped on the hillside above the Variante Bassa has to be experienced. Certainly, Hakkinen didn't enjoy their baying as he clambered sheepishly from his mangled McLaren in front of them in May 1999.

HERO OF THE TRACK

It doesn't matter to the *tifosi* what nationality their hero is, as long as he's winning for Ferrari. And so Michael Schumacher is the man they cheer for, even though Eddie Irvine was more popular before last season was out. Michael always goes well at Imola and he sent them home happy last year after a fine win, going one better than he'd managed in 1998. Michael also won here in 1994, but that didn't count to the *tifosi* as he was a Benetton driver back then.

SILVERSTONE

British Grand Prix
SILVERSTONE

Silverstone

Circuit length: **5.140km**
Race distance: **60 laps**

Woodcote
Brooklands
Copse
Luffield
Priory
Farm
Bridge
Abbey
Maggotts
Club
Becketts
Vale
Chapel
Hangar
Straight
Stowe

'99 Pole: **Hakkinen**
Winner: **Coulthard**
Timing sectors

ROUND 4   APRIL 23, 2000

Silverstone is a key part of Formula One folklore, having hosted the first World Championship Grand Prix in 1950. It's a great circuit with the Grand Prix always backed up by a strong supporting race programme.

Silverstone, 3.194 miles/5.140km. 60 laps. Lap record: Michael Schumacher (Ferrari), 1m24.475s, 136.115mph, 1997

'99 results
1 David Coulthard — McLaren
2 Eddie Irvine — Ferrari
3 Ralf Schumacher — Williams
4 Heinz-Harald Frentzen — Jordan
5 Damon Hill — Jordan
6 Pedro Diniz — Sauber

British fans are spoiled for choice, with racing every weekend from March and October at a wide variety of circuits at which they can see the stars of the future. But, come April, there is only one place to head, and that's to Silverstone, one of the cradles of world motor sport.

Silverstone hosted the first modern day Grand Prix in 1950, when inaugural World Champion Giuseppe Farina did battle with Alfa Romeo team-mate Juan Manuel Fangio on a flat and featureless layout around the perimeters of the airfield with corners marked out by oil drums.

However, writing about the British Grand Prix and mentioning only

A GAP AT THE FRONT: Mika Hakkinen lines up on pole for last year's restart, with Schumacher's grid slot left empty

PLAYING TO THE GALLERY: The smart British Racing Drivers' Club centre provides the drivers of yesteryear with excellent viewing over Brooklands and Luffield

Silverstone is misleading, as Donington Park held a Grand Prix in the 1930s when Mercedes and Auto Union thrashed the British 'opposition'. Formula One took off in the years that followed, with the British trying to break the Italian/German stranglehold as Alfa Romeo's domination was followed by Ferrari and Mercedes. When the first British win came in 1955, it was not in a British car, but a Mercedes, and at Aintree rather than Silverstone, with Stirling Moss pipping team mate Fangio.

The race alternated between Aintree and Silverstone until Brands Hatch took over from Aintree in 1964. However, Brands Hatch was dropped after 1986, which is a shame as it produced some superb races such as the one in 1985 – when it was called the Grand Prix of Europe so that Britain could host two Grands Prix that year – and Nigel Mansell scored his first Grand Prix victory.

Keep turning right...

A lap of Silverstone is all about turning right, starting with the first corner: Copse. Chopped to a 100mph bend in 1994 after Ayrton Senna's death, Copse has since been opened out, and is now taken at 150mph in fifth gear before the drivers grab sixth and hit 170mph as they jink through Maggotts and dive into the Becketts esses. This is the most exhilarating part, as it's taken at 135mph and yet offers a constant change of direction as it dives right, flicks left and then right again. Then it's hard on the power through the Chapel kink and onto the Hangar Straight and up to 190mph before hauling the car down to 110mph so the driver can turn in to the Vale dip after Stowe. Hard left at the end of this, then up and right through the double-apex Club corner and up to 180mph before the Abbey chicane. Once the fastest corner, this now slows drivers before they reach Bridge, which remains a daunting corner as the cars dive into a dip at 155mph and then turn hard right, firing up into the 'infield section'. This stretch of track gives an opportunity to gauge how close cars are to each other as the track meanders in front of the grandstands. Left at Priory, left at Brooklands, then right through Luffield and again through Woodcote and the lap is complete. It doesn't flow as it used to, but it offers some excellent viewing locations.

The pick of the pack

The best race at Silverstone since it took sole charge of the British Grand Prix was in 1987 and it's revered for the wheel-to-wheel duel between Nigel Mansell and Williams team-mate Nelson Piquet down the Hangar Straight. Six years later, there was a scrap between Damon Hill and Williams team leader Alain Prost, with Damon's engine blowing just when it looked as though he was heading for his first win. There was also a great race in 1997, with Mika Hakkinen set for his first win until his McLaren's engine blew, handing victory to Jacques Villeneuve.

The 1998 race was definitely the most confusing. Heavy rain had people aquaplaning everywhere and brought out the safety car. This wiped out Hakkinen's half minute lead. And then the race ended in confusion when new leader Michael Schumacher was penalized for passing under waved yellows and called in for his stop/go penalty after the finish. Astonishingly, he was allowed to keep his win...

Thankfully, last year's race was easier to follow, albeit having to be restarted, with the further confusion of Michael Schumacher crashing off at Stowe and breaking his right leg after the red flags had been hung out. Then Hakkinen should have won, but a faulty wheelchange scuppered his chances, leaving the way clear for Coulthard to finish ahead of Irvine, the Ferrari number two left to rue overshooting his pit on his first pitstop. Hakkinen's day was made complete when his poorly applied rear wheel eventually fell off. Perhaps the drive of the day came from Ralf Schumacher, though, as he stormed around to third in his underpowered Williams.

HERO OF THE TRACK

Ask British fans in the 1960s who they would cheer for and they were spoiled for choice. By the 1970s, James Hunt was the man. John Watson was superceeded by Nigel Mansell. And the 1990s meant Damon Hill. But Mansellmania remains the greatest memory for Silverstone's owners, Nigel's maximum attack style packing the circuit like never before. Even if they did spill over onto the track before the race was fully over...

BARCELONA

ROUND 5   MAY 7, 2000

Barcelona's Catalunya circuit is a fabulous venue — a drivers' track. But the home of the Spanish Grand Prix failed to deliver a great race in 1999. So, let's hope that it comes up with the goods this year.

Spanish Grand Prix
B A R C E L O N A

Circuit length: 4.727km
Race distance: 65 laps

Barcelona

May 7th

Banc Sabadell

La Caixa

Nissan

Campsa

Repsol

Seat Renault

Elf

'99 Pole: Hakkinen
Winner: Hakkinen

Timing sectors

Circuit de Catalunya, Barcelona, 2.937 miles/4.727km. 65 laps. Lap record: Giancarlo Fisichella (Jordan-Peugeot), 1m22.242s, 128.604mph, 1997

'99 results
1 Mika Hakkinen — McLaren
2 David Coulthard — McLaren
3 Michael Schumacher — Ferrari
4 Eddie Irvine — Ferrari
5 Ralf Schumacher — Williams
6 Jarno Trulli — Prost

Five circuits have hosted the Spanish Grand Prix over the years. The first Spanish Grand Prix was held at the round-the-houses Pedralbes circuit on the outskirts of Barcelona back in 1951. However, after a second Grand Prix there in 1954, Spain didn't host another Grand Prix until 1968 when the Jarama circuit on the outskirts of Madrid took over. This purpose-built venue's tenure of the Grand Prix was short, as a year later the scenic Montjuich Park circuit in a downtown Barcelona park took its turn. These two circuits shared the Grand Prix in an alternating pattern that continued until 1975 when the rear wing came off race leader Rolf Stommelen's Hill chassis, which vaulted the barriers and killed five spectators. That spelt the end of the Montjuich Park as a venue.

The Spanish Grand Prix has since been shared by Barcelona's

POWER DOWN: The circuit twists and climbs through the long Renault right-hander after the first corner esses

HERO OF THE TRACK

Spain has hosted a Grand Prix on and off since 1951, but it has yet to produce a race-winning driver. However, local fans at least had two home-grown heroes to cheer on last year. And both Pedro de la Rosa and Marc Gene were points-scorers before the year was out, even though they were driving for tail-end teams. So, the local fans' hopes are high that they will at some stage earn promotion to front-running teams. Only then will the population of Spain turn to Formula One in the way it does to motorcycle racing: in droves.

ALL IS STILL: This is how the teams find the Circuit de Catalunya when they test there away from the Grand Prix weekend: empty. No wonder it's so popular

stops for fresh Goodyears, while rival Olivier Panis was able to press far harder on more resilient Bridgestone rubber. Tyres weren't such an issue in 1998 as the McLarens of Mika Hakkinen and David Coulthard wiped the floor with the opposition, with Michael Schumacher the best of the rest and Benetton's Alexander Wurz the only other unlapped runner after their team-mates Eddie Irvine and Giancarlo Fisichella clashed while contesting fourth place. In 1999 , the race again went to Hakkinen ahead of Coulthard and Michael Schumacher. But the McLaren men's advantage wasn't as great as it had been in 1998 and Schumacher found himself trapped in the early laps behind Jacques Villeneuve's unusually competitive BAR.

A long, long straight

The Catalunya circuit to the north of Barcelona is now the nation's true home. Opened for racing in 1991, its layout is considered better than other modern circuits in that the designer has taken into account the fact that people like overtaking rather than processions, and designed the circuit so that the lengthy start/finish straight leads into a sharp right-hand corner approached at 190mph. Clearly, this requires heavy braking and this is where overtaking happens if a driver has been able to catch a tow from the car ahead and been able to slingshot past. And if they get this wrong, there's a huge gravel trap to catch them.

This first corner, a right-hander, is followed by a left then a long uphill right-hander. Drivers should be doing 170mph before hitting the brakes for a right-hander, Repsol, from where the track dips and feeds through the Seat left-hander, then a left kink and into the uphill left-hander that takes them up a hill to the Campsa corner at the crest. Carrying as much speed as possible over the crest, drivers should hit 180mph down the circuit's second longest straight before the double-apex left at La Caixa. From here, the track climbs back up to Banc Sabadell corner, a right-hander. The final two right-handers, running gently downhill, are crucial to a quick time as they're fifth gear corners onto that unusually long start/finish straight.

Catalunya circuit and by Jerez, with the balance recently in favour of the former. Jerez is situated in the far south of the country, between Seville and the coast. Dry and dusty, it's beautifully equipped, but too far from major centres of population to draw much of a crowd. Well, not for car racing, although Spain's love of motorbike racing does have the turnstiles spinning. The Jerez track is twisty, particularly since the introduction of a chicane following Martin Donnelly's massive accident at the corner behind the pits, Curva Ferrari. However, Jerez's claims to fame are that it produced the second closest Grand Prix finish of all time in 1986 when Ayrton Senna's Lotus edged out Nigel Mansell's Williams by 0.014 seconds after almost 200 miles, and that Michael Schumacher clashed with Jacques Villeneuve in the 1997 finale, handing the title to the Canadian who then ceded the race to Mika Hakkinen for the Finn's first Grand Prix win.

Barcelona's best

Think of Spain and you think of dry, sunny conditions. However, perhaps unluckily, rain has hit from time to time through the 1990s. And, none more so than in 1996 when Michael Schumacher blitzed the field as many others failed even to keep their cars on the track despite running at a far more conservative pace than Schumacher as the rain turned torrential.

Heavy tyre wear was the blight of many a driver's race in 1997, with winner Jacques Villeneuve nursing his Williams along between its two pit

F1 NURBURGRING

ROUND 6   MAY 21, 2000

People have said that the current Nurburgring is not a patch on the original 14-mile circuit, but the old circuit can never have provided as exciting a race as last year's European Grand Prix. Just a little rain was all that was needed...

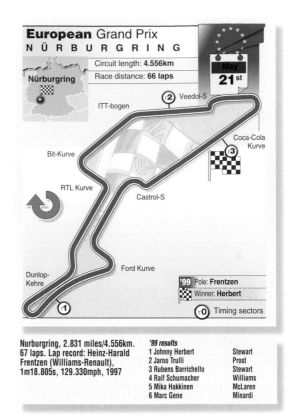

European Grand Prix
N Ü R B U R G R I N G

Circuit length: 4.556km

Race distance: 66 laps

May **21**st

Nürburgring

ITT-bogen

Veedol-S

Coca-Cola Kurve

Bit-Kurve

RTL Kurve

Castrol-S

Ford Kurve

Dunlop-Kehre

'99 Pole: **Frentzen**

Winner: **Herbert**

Timing sectors

Nurburgring, 2.831 miles/4.556km. 67 laps. Lap record: Heinz-Harald Frentzen (Williams-Renault), 1m18.805s, 129.330mph, 1997

'99 results

1 Johnny Herbert	Stewart
2 Jarno Trulli	Prost
3 Rubens Barrichello	Stewart
4 Ralf Schumacher	Williams
5 Mika Hakkinen	McLaren
6 Marc Gene	Minardi

One person, and one person alone, is responsible for Germany being allowed two Grands Prix every year and that's Michael Schumacher. Germany was a country that hadn't enjoyed sustained success in Formula One, but as soon as he started winning for Benetton in the early 1990s it was as though he had lit the blue touchpaper and this huge nation wanted to watch Formula One. With the German Grand Prix a sell-out at Hockenheim, another race was needed. So, the Nurburgring circuit that had held the nominal European Grand Prix in 1984 and the German Grand Prix in 1985 was awarded the European Grand Prix in 1995. It has held a Grand Prix every year since, either under the mantle of European Grand Prix or, once, the Luxembourg Grand Prix.

It starts with a tight right

Pedro Diniz was given every reason to remember the first corner in 1999, for it was here that his Sauber was flipped on the first lap, with its rollhoop being ripped off as it landed upside down. This right-hander is approached at 185mph and drivers need to slow to 85mph in third to get around it. Many fail, especially on the first lap as they all try and funnel their cars down onto a very narrow racing line and several invariably end up in the huge gravel trap, out of which some are able to emerge – providing they've managed not to bog down. A third-gear left-hander follows directly.

With the track dipping away, speeds of 170mph are seen before a sweeping left-hander and a tighter right. The track continues to drop away, with cars hitting 175mph before the right-hand hairpin at the bottom of the hill. Uphill out of here, through a sixth-gear left-right ess the cars reach 180mph up the climb before they need to slow for the RTL Kurve, a third gear left-hander out of which Damon Hill crashed in 1995. The third-gear right called Bit Kurve follows and then the track dips behind the paddock, with a sixth gear kink being taken at 175mph

AND HE'S OFF: Williams driver Alessandro Zanardi kicks up the dust after one of the many offs that marked every stage of last year's European Grand Prix

WIDE OPEN SPACES: Huge gravel traps separate the grandstands from the cars at Nurburgring's bottom hairpin

before the track rises again to the tight Veedol chicane where so many drivers get their line wrong every year and go for a vault over the kerbs. Finally, there's the second gear last corner, out of which drivers look to get into a position to slipstream past the car ahead at the start of the new lap.

A long, long history

Today's Nurburgring can in no way be mistaken for the circuit that hosted the German Grand Prix 22 times between 1951 and 1976. Known as the Nordschleife, it was 14 miles long with more than 100 corners around its tortuous and bucking length. However, the drivers were already making noises about it being too dangerous for Formula One use when Niki Lauda was nearly killed there in 1976 and it was decided that the Grand Prix should be moved to Hockenheim.

The current circuit was built around the pits area of the old track, echoing none of the characteristics of the Nordschleife. Instead of a narrow track winding its way through the trees, its course dotted with blind brows and steeply-banked corners, the circuit is wide, open and surrounded by gravel traps and grandstands. Yet, for all the criticism from those who hanker after the Nordschleife, it's not such a bad circuit. And it has hosted some great races since 1984, with the 1995 race standing out as Michael Schumacher tracked down Jean Alesi's Ferrari and passed it for the lead with three laps to go, to all but clinch his second world title for Benetton.

Michael Schumacher was knocked out of the race at the first corner by his own brother in 1997 and the two runaway McLaren-Mercedes both blew up within a lap of each other, handing a soft win to Jacques Villeneuve. Michael Schumacher had a far better run in 1998, but it failed to yield victory when he needed it most as he was outdriven by McLaren's Mika Hakkinen who outran Ferrari's polesitter by staying out for a longer first stint and putting in a string of blinding laps so that he emerged ahead: race over!

Last year's race was enlivened by rain and a string of drivers retiring from the lead. Jordan's Heinz-Harald Frentzen was the first of these, losing power as he accelerated away from his pitstop. David Coulthard took over, but pressed on too hard on a wet track and spun off. Ralf Schumacher took over in front but was on a two-stop strategy and this left Giancarlo Fisichella leading for Jordan, until he too slid off. Through it all came Johnny Herbert to give Stewart its maiden victory.

HERO OF THE TRACK

If he hadn't had a puncture halfway through last year's European Grand Prix at the Nurburgring, Ralf Schumacher would have become Germany's newest hero, but the Williams driver was deprived of what would have been his first win. Seen as wild when he arrived in Formula One with Jordan in 1997, he did little to disprove theories that he was all speed and no brain when he crashed at the first corner here on the opening lap that year, clashing with both his team-mate and his own brother who was gunning for the world title. But he is now seen as one of the best of the best.

MONACO

ROUND 7   JUNE 4, 2000

Monaco is a circuit like no other: it's in the heart of a town, sweeping past the casino and the harbourfront. The pit garages are little more than lock-up cupboards. But sponsors, fans and television companies absolutely love it.

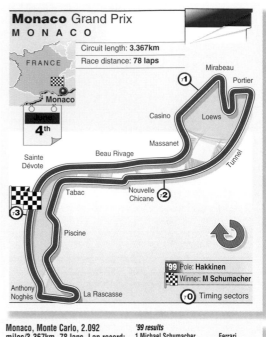

Monaco Grand Prix
M O N A C O

Circuit length: **3.367km**
Race distance: **78 laps**

FRANCE

Monaco

June
4th

Mirabeau
Portier
Casino
Loews
Massanet
Beau Rivage
Sainte Dévote
Tunnel
Tabac
Nouvelle Chicane
Piscine
Anthony Noghès
La Rascasse

'99 Pole: Hakkinen
Winner: M Schumacher
Timing sectors

Monaco, Monte Carlo, 2.092 miles/3.367km. 78 laps. Lap record: Mika Hakkinen (McLaren-Mercedes), 1m22.259s, 91.562mph, 1999

'99 results
1 Michael Schumacher	Ferrari
2 Eddie Irvine	Ferrari
3 Mika Hakkinen	McLaren
4 Heinz-Harald Frentzen	Jordan
5 Giancarlo Fisichella	Benetton
6 Alexander Wurz	Benetton

IN AN ARTIFICIAL LIGHT: Michael Schumacher adjusts his eyes as he powers through Monaco's tunnel at 150mph

To understand what the circuit at Monaco is all about, one can consider either its history or its topography, or both. So, let's start with its topography so that you can comprehend what an anachronism it really is.

A quote that is always trotted out when describing Monaco comes from Nelson Piquet. But it really is so apt: "driving a Formula One car around Monaco is like riding a bicycle around your sitting room." So, great fun, as you can imagine, but an accident waiting to happen. And any driver who has raced at Monaco has to agree, as the track is twisty, steep, and above all narrow.

Turn right at the start

The lap begins from the curving grid that bends right towards Ste Dévote, a tight right that's a really tricky corner, especially with a pack of anxious and attacking drivers on the opening lap. Indeed, it would be fine if the track was wider, but there's only one line around it and trouble is almost

ON THE HARBOURFRONT: The luxury yachts are made to pull back from the quayside during the Grand Prix just in case a car flies off at the chicane and into the water

always assured. Remember, for example, when Derek Daly clipped the car ahead of him in 1980, vaulted over it and then landed on Jean-Pierre Jarier, his Tyrrell team-mate... So, caution is required, if rarely applied.

The cars hit 160mph on the climb towards Casino Square. The left-hander at the top is blind over a crest, and a driver has to set his car up unsighted for the right-hander that runs out of the far side of Casino Square and down past the Tip-Top Bar to the ultra-tight Mirabeau right-hander. The track continues to descend down to the left-hand Loews hairpin. It's not an overtaking place, but that doesn't stop people trying.

The track continues to drop to the double-right onto the seafront at Portier. Then comes the tunnel. Dark after the light outside, it's tricky and made all the trickier by bending to the right and being taken at 150mph. Blinking in the daylight again, drivers brake hard, jink left, right, left onto the harbourside. Careering past the yachts, drivers race on towards the fast left at Tabac and funnel left, right, right, left around Piscine before jinking into the La Rascasse hairpin and up through the fiddly tight right at Anthony Noghès before accelerating hard on towards the start/finish line.

There's next to no room for mistakes. So, as you can imagine, more place changing takes place around the time of pitstops than when the drivers are threading their cars around the track. While the drivers remain ambivalent about the challenge at what is basically a low-speed circuit, sponsors adore the race as nowhere else on the calendar comes close for the art of networking. It has the harbour, the casino, the beautiful people and its own royal family.

One of the originals

Used since 1929, the circuit at Monaco has changed remarkably little, save for the start being moved away from the harbourfront and the chicane being moved closer to the exit of the tunnel. The narrowness of the track has remained the same and many races have turned into a procession as overtaking is so tricky. In spite of this, there have been some fantastic Monaco Grands Prix. None more so than in 1981 when three drivers held the lead in the

final three and a half laps before Riccardo Patrese recovered from spinning out of the lead to win. There was also Nigel Mansell's amazing pursuit of Ayrton Senna in 1992 when he did everything but climb over the top of the McLaren in his quest to push his Williams back ahead after an enforced pitstop.

Rain made the race dramatic in 1996 as Olivier Panis mastered the changing conditions best to give Ligier its first win since 1980. It was the same in 1997, as many teams were caught on the wrong tyres on a wet track. As expected in the rain, Michael Schumacher dominated for Ferrari for his third Monaco scalp in four years. The streets were made wetter still by the tears around the Stewart pit as Rubens Barrichello finished second for the team's first points.

McLaren returned to the top in 1998 when Mika Hakkinen was able to win easily once team-mate David Coulthard had retired from his tail. Giancarlo Fisichella survived a spin to finish second for Benetton ahead of Eddie Irvine's Ferrari. A moment that will stick in the mind is when Michael Schumacher barged his way past Alexander Wurz's Benetton at Loews, only for the Austrian to repass him at the next corner. But Wurz's suspension collapsed in the tunnel later in the race, probably as a result of their contact. Ferrari dominated last year when Michael Schumacher got the jump on poleman Hakkinen to lead away from the start and Eddie Irvine likewise demoted Coulthard to fourth. With the Scot retiring, Irvine attacked Hakkinen who later slipped up an escape road, clearing the way for a Ferrari one-two.

MONTREAL

ROUND 8   JUNE 18, 2000

There's something about the Circuit Gilles Villeneuve in Montreal that creates racing of great spectacle. The island circuit may look tame, but it's a real car breaker and never fails to excite the spectators.

Canadian Grand Prix
M O N T R E A L
Circuit length: 4.421km
Race distance: 69 laps

Montreal
USA

June
18th

Coin Senna

'99 Pole: M Schumacher
Winner: Hakkinen

L'Epingle

Droit du Casino

Timing sectors

Circuit Gilles Villeneuve, Montreal, 2.748 miles/4.421km. 69 laps. Lap record: Michael Schumacher (Ferrari), 1m19.379s, 124.591mph, 1998

'99 results
1 Mika Hakkinen	McLaren
2 Giancarlo Fisichella	Benetton
3 Eddie Irvine	Ferrari
4 Ralf Schumacher	Williams
5 Johnny Herbert	Stewart
6 Pedro Diniz	Sauber

Formula One and Canada have been linked in three ways since the country hosted a Grand Prix for the first time in 1967. Back then, despite a complete lack of indigenous drivers being Formula One regulars, there was simply the desire to host a Grand Prix, with local drivers renting cars for their home race.

Canada's early Grands Prix weren't held in Montreal, but on road circuits up-country at Mosport Park in Ontario and Quebec's Mont Tremblant. These races were held in autumn, and it was a wonder to behold the colour of the leaves on the trees, making the backdrop one of the most attractive in Formula One. However, neither was considered sufficiently safe as the sport advanced through the 1970s.

The second phase came when Gilles Villeneuve rose through from snowmobile racing via the junior formulae to explode onto the international scene in 1977. With the arrival of Gilles, the Canadians had a

ACROSS THE WATER: The Circuit Gilles Villeneuve is on an island just across the river from downtown Montreal

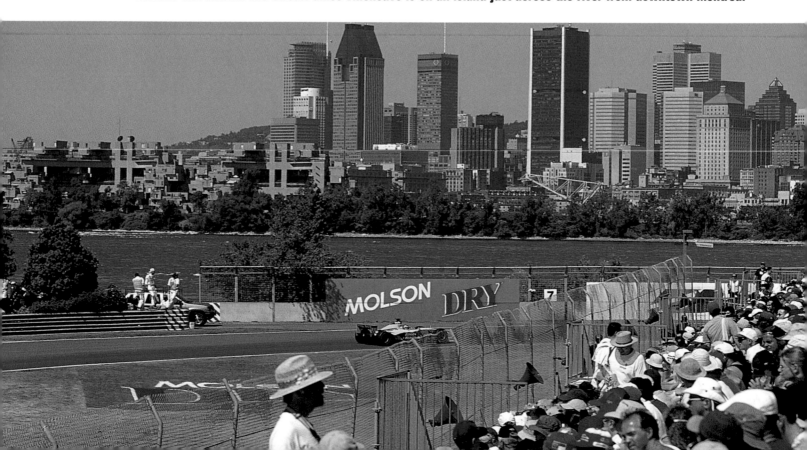

HERO OF THE TRACK

Gilles Villeneuve was a genius at the wheel, his sideways style never failing to entertain as he drove some Ferraris that clearly didn't want to go as fast as was he was making them go. A hotshot who rose to the top from snowmobile racing via Formula Atlantic before hitting Formula One, he was never a World Champion. Yet Gilles won six times, and none was as popular as when he won the first Grand Prix held in Montreal, which is why the circuit was named after him...

A GAMBLER'S GAME: Michael Schumacher had no time to stop at the casino in the background, but gambled just a tiny bit too much and crashed out of 1999's race

frontrunner to cheer and the race was moved to its current Montreal venue, with Gilles winning the first race there in 1978. Not surprisingly, Formula One hit new heights of popularity in Canada on the back of his success, drawing ever more of the Canadian populace away from their interest in ice hockey. Tragically, Gilles died in 1982 while trying to qualify for the Belgian Grand Prix, and Canada lost interest again, its new-found race fans looking more to the United States' Indycar championship.

The third phase of Canadian interest came with the arrival of Gilles' son, Jacques, who'd already made people sit up and pay attention by winning the 1995 Indycar title before joining the Formula One circus with Williams. It seemed that everyone in Quebec wanted to see Jacques win in 1996 on the circuit named after his late father. And he came close, but could do nothing to stop team-mate Damon Hill from winning.

Hemmed in on all sides

Built on the site of the EXPO 67 display, the circuit sends car after car into retirement as its bumps and tight corners stress the moving parts like nowhere else. The track is on a long, thin island on the St Lawrence River, pinned in on one side by the Olympic rowing basin and by the river on the other, leaving very little space for the track and even less for the grandstands.

The run to the first corner includes a right kink before the track goes left. And it's here that the trouble invariably happens on the opening lap, as you will undoubtedly remember from that much-used piece of footage of the start in 1998 when Alexander Wurz barrel-rolled his Benetton into

the huge gravel trap, with cars scattering in avoidance.

The track then feeds into a right-hand hairpin, the Virage Senna. From here, the track opens out into a series of esses and chicanes between the ever-present concrete barriers before touching 180mph on the curving back straight. The Pits Hairpin is reached after negotiating a second chicane and another kinking straight. This is the circuit's best overtaking spot, but it's best-known as the point where Nigel Mansell waved to the fans when leading on the final lap in 1991, only to stall and let Nelson Piquet through to win... Actually, the hairpin is nowhere near the pits and the drivers must blast back to the pit area down the circuit's longest straight, hitting 190mph before the final chicane, a tight right-left that saw so many drivers come to grief in 1999.

Those concrete walls...

The surrounding concrete walls are generally bounced off by errant cars, but in 1997 Olivier Panis's Prost hit the barriers at 150mph and he broke both legs. This brought out the safety car and, at that same moment, race leader David Coulthard stalled in the pits and this allowed Michael Schumacher to claim a surprise victory when the race was halted four laps later. Mind you, many local fans had already long since left, as Jacques Villeneuve had ended his race against the wall on the second lap. Typically, for Montreal, this didn't make him the first out of the race, as Jan Magnussen, Eddie Irvine and Mika Hakkinen had all beaten him to that fate...

In 1998, Wurz was launched over Jean Alesi's Sauber at the start, his Benetton flipping into the gravel trap and forcing a restart. With both McLarens retiring, Michael Schumacher dominated for Ferrari, but only after he'd left the pits in a rash move that pitched Heinz-Harald Frentzen's Williams into retirement.

The walls played their most prolific role last year when the stretch of concrete on the exit of the final chicane was struck by Ricardo Zonta, Damon Hill, Michael Schumacher and Villeneuve, all retiring on the spot. Then Frentzen thumped a tyre barrier at the first chicane four laps from the finish and elevated Giancarlo Fisichella into second behind Hakkinen, with Irvine starring as he raced back to third after a clash with Coulthard earlier in the race at the first corner.

MAGNY-COURS

KNOW THE TRACKS

82

ROUND 9   JULY 2, 2000

Magny-Cours is not the most popular circuit visited during the European summer. Yet, for all its seeming lack of soul, it has produced some great racing, especially into its Adelaide hairpin.

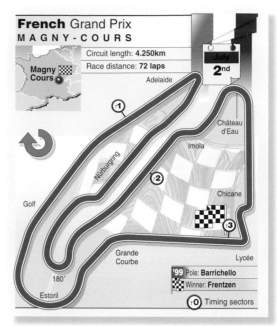

French Grand Prix
M A G N Y - C O U R S

Circuit length:	**4.250km**
Race distance:	**72 laps**

'99 Pole: **Barrichello**

Winner: **Frentzen**

Timing sectors

Magny-Cours, 2.641 miles/4.250km. 72 laps. Lap record: David Coulthard (McLaren), 1m17.523s, 123.355mph, 1998

'99 results

1	Heinz-Harald Frentzen	Jordan
2	Mika Hakkinen	McLaren
3	Rubens Barrichello	Stewart
4	Ralf Schumacher	Williams
5	Michael Schumacher	Ferrari
6	Eddie Irvine	Ferrari

FULL SPEED AHEAD: The front half of the field filters through Grande Courbe on the opening lap in last year's race

Modern it may be. Purpose-built it most certainly is. But popular it is not. Yes, we're talking about Magny-Cours, a circuit that seemed to spring from nowhere in 1991 to host the French Grand Prix. Well, not from nowhere exactly, but it had been merely a club circuit until the government suddenly granted a healthy development budget for reasons of political expediency.

This transformation would have been remarkable in any country, but it was all the more so as it happened in France, the country that invented motorsport, having been home to the first ever motor race in 1894 when a race was held from Paris to Rouen. France remained a major player until the Second World War, after which the Italians took over, then the

Germans in the 1950s and finally the British in the 1960s.

The first circuit to host the French Grand Prix in the modern era (that is to say post-1950) was Reims, on an almost triangular course of public roads. Races at Reims were famed for drivers hunting as a pack as they attempted to slipstream onto the tail of the car ahead. Interspersed in the same period from the early 1950s to the late 1960s were Grands Prix at Rouen-les-Essarts, a trickier track through the trees just outside Rouen, and a one-off at Le Mans. Perhaps the greatest track to have hosted the French Grand Prix was used from 1965. This was the circuit high on the hill above Clermont-Ferrand. Dipping and twisting through fast and often blind corners, it was a classic. But after 1972 it was adjudged too dangerous.

SUPER SUITES: The hospitality suites with balconies above the pitlane afford the guests a fantastic view of the grid

The flat and fast Paul Ricard circuit just inland from the Riviera was introduced in 1971, with the Grand Prix staying there until 1990, with forays to the tighter but equally popular Dijon-Prenois circuit up until 1984. The Grand Prix is rumoured to be returning to Paul Ricard in the very near future, taking over from Magny-Cours.

The rise of Magny-Cours

Magny-Cours had the good fortune to be located in a backward rural area. The then president, François Mitterand, decided that it should be transformed into the centre of technical excellence for French motorsport and thus attract high-quality employment into the region – to say nothing of the money that comes when the Formula One circus pays its annual visit.

The best corner is at the start of the lap, this a combination of the fast, but tightening, Grande Courbe left-hander into the long, long Estoril right-hander. And it's essential to get this right for a quick exit onto the back straight, as not only is this long, but it leads into the principal overtaking point: the Adelaide hairpin. This is located at the top of the hill and the braking for the right-hand hairpin is severe, as the drivers have to drop from 180mph. Some go in fast and are slow out, while others appear to have been too cautious but then get the power down more effectively on the exit and go back in front again.

The track twists down through the Nurburgring esse to a more open hairpin, then heads uphill again through the fast Imola esse into Chateau d'Eau. Out of this right-hander, the track then drops down to the tightest chicane. Then, out of this chicane there's Lycée, a tight right-hander onto the pit straight where the cars often brush the pitwall on the exit.

Improved by rain

Rain has played a role in most of the recent French Grands Prix. In 1997, there was a German clean sweep at the front of the grid, with Michael Schumacher taking pole ahead of Heinz-Harald Frentzen and brother Ralf.

While Ralf dropped back to sixth, Michael led Heinz-Harald home in a processional race that was brought to life by a shower in the closing laps.

It was expected to be a race of McLaren domination in 1998, but Michael Schumacher qualified on the front row alongside Mika Hakkinen and took the lead when the race was restarted. Michael's team-mate Eddie Irvine shot into second, letting Michael escape as he held up the McLarens. Hakkinen spun at the Lycée bend after passing Irvine, falling back behind again, while David Coulthard hit refuelling problems and fell to sixth.

Last year there was rain of the sort that would have had Noah building an ark. And, timing his run in qualifying just right, Rubens Barrichello placed his Stewart on pole. Coulthard was the class act in the race though, but retired from the lead, while Hakkinen spun down to seventh and Michael Schumacher also led but slowed with a problem. And, by guessing the conditions right and putting in enough fuel not to have to stop twice, Frentzen raced through to win for Jordan ahead of the fast-recovering Hakkinen. The rain made the race.

HERO OF THE TRACK

No disrespect is meant to Jean Alesi, but when one thinks of great French drivers of the 1990s, one still thinks of Alain Prost first, even though he was also France's top driver through the 1980s as well. However, Alain's tally of four world titles – in 1985, 1986 and 1989 for McLaren and in 1993 for Williams – puts 'The Professor' streets clear. He even won his home Grand Prix six times, whereas Alesi may have led his home race, but he's never won it.

A1-RING

Austrian Grand Prix
S P I E L B E R G

Circuit length: 4.319km
Race distance: 71 laps

July 16th

A1-Ring

A1 Kurve

Jochen Rindt Kurve

Castrol Kurve

Power Horse Kurve

Gösser Kurve

Niki Lauda Kurve

Remus Kurve

'99 Pole: Hakkinen

Winner: **Irvine**

Timing sectors

A1-Ring, 2.684 miles/4.319km. 71 laps. Lap record: Jacques Villeneuve (McLaren-Mercedes), 1m11.814s, 122.60mph, 1997

'99 results		
1 Eddie Irvine		Ferrari
2 David Coulthard		McLaren
3 Mika Hakkinen		McLaren
4 Heinz-Harald Frentzen		Jordan
5 Alexander Wurz		Benetton
6 Pedro Diniz		Sauber

ROUND 10   JULY 16, 2000

The A1-Ring was derided when it was opened in 1997 for being a shadow of the Osterreichring, over which it was built. But it has provided three cracking races out of three, so it can't be all bad.

The reason that people were so sad when they first set eyes on the A1-Ring was that its new layout finally buried one of their favourite circuit of old: the Osterreichring. Not only did it offer a magnificent challenge to the drivers, but it offered unrivalled viewing potential for the spectators too. And it hosted some classic races, as shown in 1982 when Elio de Angelis's Lotus was pushed all the way to the finish line by Keke Rosberg's Williams, with Elio holding on to win by just 0.05 seconds. While the A1-Ring was on the same site, its layout is one shorn of the best bits of the old circuit, with the fast, open sweepers replaced by slower, tighter corners, as has happened at several other venues.

For all this, though, the creation of the A1-Ring was the only way of ensuring that Austria regained a place on the World Championship calendar after a ten-year break. And, of course, the Styrrian mountain scenery remains as glorious as before.

Five rights and two lefts

If people try to tell you that Formula One circuits are all built on flat land, like at Silverstone, tell them they are wrong, as anyone who tries to walk

A FLIGHT OF ARROWS: The Arrows duo of Pedro de la Rosa and Toranosuke Takagi brake for the uphill Remus Kurve

HERO OF THE TRACK

Of all the great Austrian drivers, it's Niki Lauda who stands clear at the top of the pile. Seen as wealthy rather than quick, he bought his way in to Formula One. But, once there, soon impressed and landed a drive with Ferrari in 1974, turning around a team in turmoil and winning the 1975 and 1977 titles before joining Brabham. After a three-year break, he joined McLaren in 1982 and won a third title in 1984 when he finally won his home Grand Prix at his tenth attempt.

THE RACE OF HIS LIFE: Eddie Irvine puts his Ferrari's hammer down out of the Remus Kurve during his mid-race sprint that earned him a vital victory last year

Surprise winners, surprising races

Ever since the first Austrian Grand Prix in 1964, the event has produced numerous exciting races and encouraged some great Austrian talent, such as Jochen Rindt, Niki Lauda and Gerhard Berger. However, there was a spell in the mid-1970s when it produced first-time winners three years in succession, namely Vittorio Brambilla, John Watson and Alan Jones between 1975 and 1977. The little-fancied Italian's surprise success in 1975 remains the most memorable of these as a deluge turned the race into a lottery and he stayed calm in his orange works March while those around him spun off. And he was still in front when the race was stopped early. On seeing the chequered flag he got over-excited on the slowing-down lap and crashed... Watson's win for Penske in 1976 and Jones's success for Shadow in 1977 – both the only wins for these respective teams – were rather more controlled.

The A1-Ring's first race, in 1997, threatened to revive this tradition of producing first-time winners, with Formula One rookie Jarno Trulli looking set for victory for the new Prost team until he fell behind Jacques Villeneuve's Williams during a pitstop sequence and then had to retire when his engine blew.

The following year's race was a McLaren one-two, even though David Coulthard had to fight his way from the back to second after being pitched into a spin on the opening lap and having to pit for a new nose. Michael Schumacher recovered from having to pit to repair damage done by a huge airborne moment out of the Jochen Rindt Kurve and was able to grab third when his team-mate Eddie Irvine surprisingly had to slow with 'brake problems'.

Last year's race was extraordinary from the moment that Coulthard tipped Hakkinen out of the lead at the second corner on the opening lap, to the moment that Irvine took a later pitstop than Coulthard and emerged in a lead he was to keep to the finish to show that Ferrari could win with Michael Schumacher convalescing at home. Hakkinen, who fell to last, tigered through to third.

from the startline at the A1-Ring up to the first corner will attest. It's steep. And, on a flying lap, the ascent is taken at 185mph with heavy braking before the brow to the first corner, a tight right taken in second gear. There's then a long 185mph climb, with a kink and then a kick-up at the end to the Remus Kurve. Taken in second gear, it's a second-gear hairpin that has seen plenty of action over the course of its three-year history, with Jean Alesi's leap over Eddie Irvine's Ferrari in 1997 still the most spectacular.

The drivers then blast down a gentle descent, again hitting 185mph before having to brake for the Gosser Kurve, a third gear double-apex right-hander in place of the faster Boschkurve of old. The track doubles back across to Niki Lauda Kurve, a dropping fourth-gear left-hander, and then dives down to Power Horse Kurve, another fourth-gear left-hander before drivers have to power up and over a crest behind the paddock before dropping down again to the penultimate corner – Jochen Rindt Kurve – a testing right-hander where Michael Schumacher went for a cross-country ride in 1998 and on down a short slope to the A1 Kurve, a simple, fifth-gear right-hander onto the bottom of the start/finish straight.

All in all, the A1-Ring is a compact circuit, and certainly not blessed with the flowing majesty of the Osterreichring. But, that said, it does still offer at least three potential overtaking points. The first of these is under braking for the first corner. The next is at the second corner. And the third is at the third, showing that a high-speed entry into a slow corner is still the best way to offer overtaking.

HOCKENHEIM

ROUND 11   JULY 30, 2000

Hockenheim is a circuit of two parts. One part is slow and twisty in front of massive grandstands. The other is flat-out through a forest, with the cars hunting in large slipstreaming packs at speeds of over 200mph.

German Grand Prix
H O C K E N H E I M

Circuit length: 6.823km
Race distance: 45 laps

Hockenheimring

30th

Jim Clark Kurve
Ostkurve
Ayrton Senna Kurve
Nordkurve
Sachs
Agip Kurve
Südkurve

'99 Pole: **Hakkinen**
Winner: **Irvine**
Timing sectors

Hockenheim, 4.239 miles/6.823km. 45 laps. Lap record: David Coulthard (McLaren-Mercedes), 1m45.270s, 144.985mph, 1999

'99 results	
1 Eddie Irvine	Ferrari
2 Mika Salo	Ferrari
3 Heinz-Harald Frentzen	Jordan
4 Ralf Schumacher	Williams
5 David Coulthard	McLaren
6 Olivier Panis	Prost

FERRARIS TO THE FORE: Eddie Irvine raced to victory last year ahead of Michael Schumacher's stand-in Mika Salo

GIANT GRANDSTANDS: The Benettons lead the midfield through the Sachs Kurve in the 'stadium' section of the track

The German Grand Prix was held at the Nurburgring from 1951 to 1976, apart from a visit to Avus in 1959 and one to Hockenheim in 1970. At over 14 miles in length, the Nurburgring offered over 100 corners, with blind brows and banked bends to keep the drivers on their toes and the spectators entertained. But the circuit held its final Grand Prix in 1976 when Niki Lauda nearly lost his life there. Formula One had outgrown it and the circuit was relegated to holding races for national categories.

The German Grand Prix came to Hockenheim for good in 1977. And, even though nine years had passed, the circuit was still strongly associated with the death of reigning World Champion Jim Clark in a Formula Two race in 1968.

Fortunately, with every passing year, the memory of Clark recedes, helped by the fact that there have been some great races, exciting slipstreaming affairs with furious ducking and diving as the pack splits up at the chicanes and those at the rear try to slingshot past their opponents.

In 1985, Hockenheim was dropped for a year when the Grand Prix returned to the Nurburgring albeit not to the original track – the Nordschleife – but to a modern circuit built around the old pits. Even more so than with the Osterreichring's transformation to the A1-Ring, there is next to no connection between old and new, with the track comprising constant-radius corners, having said goodbye to its atmosphere.

Fast and slow

Hockenheim's first corner is a fourth gear right-hander, where Jacques Villeneuve speared off in last year's race after clashing with Pedro Diniz on the opening lap. Then it's a flat-out blast up to the first chicane, the Jim Clark Kurve, hitting close on 220mph. Well, the cars blessed with more powerful engines do as they run with almost no angle on their wings. There is a right-left second gear chicane, then the drivers accelerate back up to 210mph before they reach the far end of the loop and the Ost Kurve chicane. This is another right-left sequence, again with meaty kerbs that are best avoided. An arcing right as the drivers get the power down feeds onto the straight that heads back towards the stadium. Halfway along its length, it is interrupted by the final chicane, the Ayrton Senna Kurve, which differs in that it's left then right.

The cars remain out of sight of the people in the grandstands in the "stadium" section until they burst back out of the trees at Agip Kurve, arriving back into the infield through the sharp right-hander that Mika Hakkinen spun through last year. Some passing moves are pulled off at Agip, but many prefer to dive past into the left-handed second-gear Sachs Kurve. There's then a left kink and a double-apex third-gear right onto the

start/finish straight. When the 120,000 people packed into the grandstands in Hockenheim's "stadium" section cheer, the drivers can hear them over their engine noise. It's impressive, particularly if you're a German driver and they are cheering for you, but it can also be daunting if your name is Damon Hill and you're attempting to stand in the way of Michael Schumacher's bid for another world title.

Berger's happy hunting ground

Gerhard Berger was a driver who shone at Hockenheim. For example, in 1994, he ended Ferrari's longest run without a win here. Two years later, Gerhard was all set to give Benetton its first win since Schumacher left the team at the end of the previous season when his engine blew with three laps to go. In 1997, he came back from illness, his father's death and the news that he had no future with Benetton to start on pole, set fastest lap and win.

Michael Schumacher had his worst run of the 1998 season at Hockenheim, his Ferrari off the pace as Mika Hakkinen and David Coulthard powered into the distance in their McLarens. Schumacher finished fifth, behind the improving Williams and Jordan of Jacques Villeneuve and Damon Hill respectively. There was very little cheering in the grandstands.

Last year's race produced a surprise result, with Hakkinen seeming to have it in the bag until his refuelling rig failed to work and he fell to fourth place. But that was nothing as he then had a huge blowout and was fortunate to walk away from the ensuing crash. And, with Coulthard having been given a stop/go penalty, this left the way clear for Ferrari stand-in Mika Salo to pull over and let Eddie Irvine through to lead home a Ferrari one-two.

HERO OF THE TRACK

Michael Schumacher is still the driver the Germans pack into the huge grandstands cheer for. After all, he has been a World Champion twice and a championship contender in every other year since 1996. However, he has thus far only won the German Grand Prix once. And now he is facing a challenge for German support from two of his own, namely Heinz-Harald Frentzen and his own brother Ralf. So the Germans, long a nation without a frontrunner to cheer for, now have three.

HUNGARORING

ROUND 12   AUGUST 13, 2000

Fifteen years ago, nobody would have linked Formula One with Hungary. However, since 1986 the Hungaroring has been a stable fixture, offering some wonderful spectating if little real overtaking.

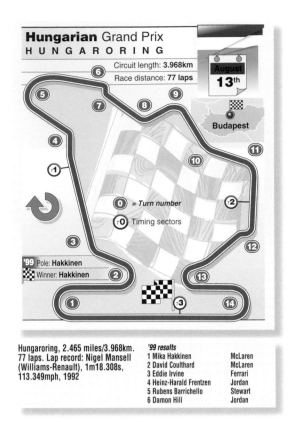

Hungarian Grand Prix
HUNGARORING

Circuit length: **3.968km**
Race distance: **77 laps**

August 13th

Budapest

0 = Turn number

0 Timing sectors

'99 Pole: Hakkinen
Winner: Hakkinen

Hungaroring, 2.465 miles/3.968km. 77 laps. Lap record: Nigel Mansell (Williams-Renault), 1m18.308s, 113.349mph, 1992

'99 results
1	Mika Hakkinen	McLaren
2	David Coulthard	McLaren
3	Eddie Irvine	Ferrari
4	Heinz-Harald Frentzen	Jordan
5	Rubens Barrichello	Stewart
6	Damon Hill	Jordan

ALWAYS IN CONTROL: A vast army of Finnish fans roared themselves hoarse as Mika Hakkinen dominated in his McLaren last year, leading the race from start to finish

When it was announced that a Grand Prix would be held in Hungary in 1986, people were surprised. After all, wasn't Hungary still a communist country? However, what emerged was the first clear sign that Formula One's organizers had an eye fixed on markets new and were no longer prepared to have a World Championship that was basically a (western) European championship with a few fly-away races tacked on. No, Formula One's big hitters were going after a whole new audience, going for countries where cigarette advertising was likely to remain unrestricted for years to come. So, enter Hungary.

Rolling hills outside Budapest provide the setting for the Hungaroring, a circuit that offers better viewing than any since Brands Hatch was dropped after 1986. And, like Brands Hatch, the Hungaroring is blessed with a natural amphitheatre as the track spans both sides of a valley and the dip in between, offering fantastic spectating from almost every vantage point.

Narrow and twisty

A lap of the Hungaroring starts high on one of the two side-slopes of the valley, with the start/finish straight towered over by a natural grandstand that runs its length. Drivers hit 180mph as the track dips into the first corner before they brake hard into a tight right-hander that continues to drop away from entry to exit as it turns back on itself. This is followed by a short straight under an access road and then a downhill left-hander that leads into a dipping right-hander. From here, it's hard on the power down the hill to the bottom of the valley with cars hitting 175mph before climbing up the other side and kinking left. The long right-hander at the top – where Eddie Irvine ran wide and lost second place last year – leads into a twisty section with a chicane followed by a left and right until it reaches left-hand Turn Ten and drops away through Turn 11 and on down to the bottom of the dip before climbing again through Turn 12 and the tighter Turns 13 and 14, the tighter one a long third gear right-hander opening out onto the start/finish straight. So, a good exit speed is necessary if a driver wants to get into the slipstream of the car ahead down the straight for a potential passing move into the first corner.

DOWN AND RIGHT: Mika Hakkinen leads the field into the first corner, where the track dips sharply away to the right

Overtaking possibilities are hard to come by on this tight, twisty track, with passing most likely during the many pitstops necessitated by the abrasive, tyre-destroying surface. Indeed, the run down to the first corner offers the only passing opportunity, as long as the following driver can get enough of a tow to slingshot past. The drivers, however, reckon that the circuit's low-speed nature means that they can have a stab at passing at numerous points without taking too much of a risk. What they have to watch out for, though, is heat exhaustion, as this land-locked country can be sweltering at the time of its Grand Prix slot in August.

A who's who of winners

Nelson Piquet was the first driver to win the Hungarian Grand Prix, doing so for Williams ahead of Ayrton Senna's Lotus, with the rest a lap and more behind. He repeated the feat the following year. Then Senna hit top spot in 1988, finishing half a second ahead of McLaren team-mate Alain Prost. By now the Hungarian Grand Prix was well and truly established. But, in the race's short history, the Hungaroring has also seen Nigel Mansell clinching the World Championship in 1992 by finishing second behind Ayrton Senna, and Damon Hill scoring his first Grand Prix win 12 months later.

Hill nearly won there for a third time in 1997, this time for Arrows rather than Williams in a performance that turned the form books on their head as he qualified third, hunted down and passed Michael Schumacher's Ferrari for the lead before dominating as his Bridgestone tyres worked supremely in the summer heat. But then, with three laps to go, his gearbox started to pack up, and former Williams team-mate Jacques Villeneuve passed him halfway around the final lap.

Perhaps the greatest showing there came in 1998 when Ferrari's Ross Brawn guided Michael Schumacher to victory over the superior McLarens by putting the German onto a three-stop strategy. It was a close-run thing, but Schumacher drove every lap as though he was on a flier in qualifying, and it worked. His victory counted for double as Mika Hakkinen faltered with a suspension problem and could finish only sixth.

Last year's race was all about Hakkinen as he led from start to finish, leaving Irvine – buoyed by consecutive wins in the Austrian and German Grands Prix – to resist Coulthard for second. However, he didn't manage it, falling to third after an off-track moment.

HERO OF THE TRACK

Damon Hill won 22 Grands Prix, and was twice victorious at the Hungaroring, a circuit that suited his precise style. But he has even more reason to like the place than you would expect, for his win here for Williams in 1993 was his first, while his 1995 win put his championship challenge back on track as Michael Schumacher faltered. Damon then nearly pulled off the surprise of the decade in 1997 when he came within a lap of winning for Arrows before his gearbox failed and he fell to second. Then, in 1999, he scored here in a year in which he found points hard to come by.

SPA-FRANCORCHAMPS

ROUND 13   AUGUST 27, 2000

Spa-Francorchamps is the world's most magnificent circuit. Not only does it enjoy a beautiful setting, but it provides the drivers with their biggest challenge of the year. And then there's the weather...

Belgian Grand Prix
SPA FRANCORCHAMPS

Circuit length: 6.968km
Race distance: 44 laps

August 27th

Francorchamps

Les Combes · Malmedy · Rivage · Kemmel · Pouhon · Radillon · Fagnes · Eau Rouge · Blanchimont · Stavelot · Bus Stop Chicane · La Source

'99 Pole: **Hakkinen**
Winner: **Coulthard**
Timing sectors

Spa-Francorchamps, 4.350 miles/6.968km. 44 laps. Lap record: Alain Prost (Williams-Renault), 1m51.095s, 140.424mph, 1993

'99 results

1 David Coulthard	McLaren
2 Mika Hakkinen	McLaren
3 Heinz-Harald Frentzen	Jordan
4 Eddie Irvine	Ferrari
5 Ralf Schumacher	Williams
6 Damon Hill	Jordan

THE BIGGEST TEST: The sharply rising stretch of track from Eau Rouge to Raidillon is the trickiest in Formula One. Just ask the BAR drivers who crashed there in '99

Ayrton Senna was stunning in 1992 when he lapped as fast on slicks in the rain as most frontrunners could manage on treaded tyres. However, his gamble didn't pay off and he failed to make it five consecutive wins as victory went instead to Michael Schumacher.

Schumacher continues to be the man to beat, and his victory in 1997 emphasised his genius as he sussed the changing weather before the start and powered clear. He looked to have done the same again in the wet in 1998, but he hit David Coulthard when the McLaren driver slowed to let himself be lapped. The race went to Damon Hill, giving Jordan its first win. However, the image that will remain is the accident triggered by Coulthard on the exit of La Source on the first lap that involved 13 cars.

Last year's race was sorted at the first corner when Coulthard got there ahead of pole-sitting team-mate Hakkinen. They touched, but no damage was done and the Scot raced clear to victory ahead of a disgruntled Finn.

Watch out for Eau Rouge

The grid is not only on an uphill stretch, but it's gently curving, giving those at the back a problem seeing the starting lights. And then there's the first corner, the La Source hairpin, scene of much wheel-banging. Tight on the way in, luckily it's wide on the exit before the drivers have to plunge downhill past the old pits to Eau Rouge. This is the most awe-inspiring corner the drivers meet all year, as the downhill slope snaps through a left-right esse into a steep ascent taken in sixth. The track crests the slope and immediately bends left at Raidillon. There have been some major accidents here, such as when Alessandro Zanardi crashed his Lotus in 1993 and then Jacques Villeneuve both in 1998 and again last year when British American Racing team-mate Ricardo Zonta also got in on the act, amazingly without injury.

It's crucial to get a good run through Eau Rouge and Raidillon, as there's then a long straight up to the esses at Les Combes. And It's here that much overtaking is done by those who manage to get a tow and slingshot past at close on 200mph. The track cuts away through a right-left esse, then dips to the right-handed Rivage. From here, the track drops away, diving through a left-handed kink and on down to Pouhon. This is a mighty corner, as it's an off-camber double-apex left-hander taken at 150mph. The Fagnes sweepers are next and take the track to its lowest point where it rejoins the original track at Stavelot corner, out of which the drivers are travelling at 150mph before continuing to accelerate up the hill through the flat-out left at Blanchimont and on up to 200mph before arriving at the Bus Stop. This set of chicanes – a left-right followed by a right-left – jars as it's so out of character with the rest of the lap, but it's spectacular as the drivers use the kerbs. From the exit of Bus Stop, the drivers negotiate the left-hand kink onto the start/finish straight then start thinking about Eau Rouge all over again...

LOOKING BACK: The glorious view from Raidillon, looking down to Eau Rouge and on up past the old pits to the La Source hairpin at the top of the hill in the distance

The Spa-Francorchamps circuit is blessed with a handful of the world's leading corners. It nestles in the Ardennes hills on the edge of the village of Francorchamps up the hill from the spa town of Spa, and is glorious for every one of the four miles of its length. Yet, the current circuit isn't a patch on the original that kept going at Les Combes before dipping into the next valley and following a triangular course – almost all of it taken flat-out with nothing between the drivers and the trees – before rejoining today's circuit at Stavelot corner. Mighty it most definitely was, safe it most definitely was not. Whatever the layout, one factor that always adds a twist is the weather, something that is fickle in the Ardennes. Particularly when the nine-mile long original circuit was used, there would often be rain at one end of the track while it would be dry at the other.

Victory only to the great

Spa-Francorchamps hasn't always been the home of the Belgian Grand Prix, as when it was considered too dangerous after 1970, the race was given to the Flemish half of Belgium in 1972, when it was held at Nivelles. It moved to another Flemish circuit, Zolder, in 1973. After Nivelles had a second shot in 1974, the race was given back to Zolder which kept it until Gilles Villeneuve lost his life there in 1982. And so the race returned to a revamped Spa-Francorchamps in 1983 and, apart from one last go at Zolder in 1984, it has been there ever since.

Spa-Francorchamps has rewarded only the top drivers with victory.

HERO OF THE TRACK

Belgium is still searching for a driver to start to make the impact on the world scene that Jacky Ickx did in the 1960s and early 1970s. A former motorcycle trials champion, he converted to racing cars, winning eight Grands Prix for Ferrari and Brabham and being runner-up in the World Championship both in 1969 and 1970. Jacky was never more sublime than in the wet, something that is always useful at Spa-Francorchamps. Ironically, he never won at his home circuit. He also won the Le Mans 24 Hours six times.

MONZA

ROUND 14   SEPTEMBER 10, 2000

Monza is a temple of Formula One, having held a Grand Prix every year bar one since the World Championship started in 1950. It's also the spiritual home of Ferrari's most passionate fans, the *tifosi*.

Italian Grand Prix
M O N Z A

Circuit length: **5.770km**
Race distance: **53 laps**

Curva Grande

Variante della Roggia

Curva di Lesmos

Rettifilo Tribune

Curva del Serraglio

Curva del Vialone

Variante Ascari

September **10th**

'99 **Pole: Hakkinen**
Winner: Frentzen

Curva Parabolica

Timing sectors

Monza, 3.585 miles/5.770km. 53 laps. Lap record: Mika Hakkinen (McLaren-Mercedes), 1m24.808s, 152.198mph, 1997

'99 results
1 Heinz-Harald Frentzen	Jordan
2 Ralf Schumacher	Williams
3 Mika Salo	Ferrari
4 Rubens Barrichello	Stewart
5 David Coulthard	McLaren
6 Eddie Irvine	Ferrari

Motor sport has ebbed and flowed, technical innovations have revolutionized and been superseded, but Monza remains an integral part. Its famous banked bends are no longer used, having been dropped in 1961, and lie in disrepair alongside the current circuit. But that's not the only glance into Monza's rich past that is evident when you visit its glorious parkland setting north of Milan, as its old control tower remains, along with the wonderful little shops in the paddock, looking as though time has stood still.

The vast majority of those packing the grandstands at Monza and lining every inch of fence around the track are *tifosi*, anxious to soak up

SHOWING THEIR COLOURS: The *tifosi* shout and wave only for their beloved Ferraris when the circus visits Monza

TRUE COLOURS: The *tifosi* show off the world's largest flag for the world's most popular team: Ferrari. But the famous Prancing Horse failed to prance at Monza in '99

everything to do with any matter Ferrari. Come what may, for a Ferrari to win is paramount and it ranks higher in their esteem even than victory for an Italian driving for another team. So, since he joined Ferrari from Benetton, Michael Schumacher has gone from public enemy to a saint-like standing thanks to turning Ferrari around. And Eddie Irvine's popularity went through the roof last summer when Schumacher broke a leg and he became their new number one.

Racing at 210mph

A lap of Monza is all about flat-out straights and sweeping corners broken by a handful of chicanes. With the lap record standing at 151.6mph, it's fast. Indeed, the cars hit 210mph at three different points. So, think what speeds today's cars would be reaching if it wasn't for the chicanes. It wasn't just speeds that the chicanes kept in check, though, but the slipstreaming packs. And this is a huge shame, as never again will we witness a race like the one in 1971 in which BRM's Peter Gethin won at a race average of 150.755mph after catching a pack of cars on the final lap and nipping past to win by 0.01 seconds from Ronnie Peterson's March, with the next three cars home covered by 0.61 seconds.

Sadly, when cars run close together today they don't have the opportunity or the aerodynamics to take advantage of the car ahead and so it leads to processional races such as the one in 1997 when David Coulthard won for McLaren by a short nose from Jean Alesi's Benetton, but only after getting ahead thanks to a slicker pitstop. Indeed, there was probably more overtaking on the final lap of the 1971 Italian GP than there was all race in 1997, even though the top-five were covered by 6.5 seconds.

A Ferrari one-two for Schumacher and Eddie Irvine in 1998 was the race that will be remembered by the *tifosi*, as it put Schumacher level with McLaren's Mika Hakkinen with two races to go. By rights, the race should have belonged to Coulthard, but his McLaren's engine blew when he was leading and Schumacher passed Hakkinen for the lead on the same lap when they were unsighted by smoke. Hakkinen was closing in again when he spun and Irvine and Ralf Schumacher demoted him to fourth.

Ralf Schumacher was on the podium again last year, this time having finished second in his Williams. But there was nothing he could do about Heinz-Harald Frentzen who won for Jordan after Hakkinen threw the race by spinning out of the lead. This ought to have helped Hakkinen's title

rival, Irvine, but he could finish only sixth on a day when his new number two Mika Salo raced to third.

Chopped and changed

The layout of today's circuit is not dissimilar to the one used in 1950, albeit with its flow spoiled by the chicanes that became part of the scenery in 1972 to check escalating speeds. The first chicane, which is actually one chicane followed by another, is reached on the run to what had been the first corner, the right-hand Curva Grande. The cars have to be hauled down from 215mph to 60mph to get through. But, even with this, Curva Grande remains fast, as it's still taken in fifth gear at 175mph. Without the chicane, the mind boggles at what speeds would be recorded.

The cars keep accelerating until they have to brake from 210mph to negotiate the left-right Variante della Roggia that slows their progress into the two Lesmo right-handers that are exciting enough to keep the adrenaline pumping. The cars then fire off down a kinked straight under the old banked circuit and into the Variante Ascari. After this third-gear chicane, the drivers get back onto the power and hit 210mph down the back straight before taking the 180-degree Parabolica onto the start/finish straight.

With much of the lap spent at such high speed, it's inevitable that there will be major accidents, and few have been as spectacular as the one survived by Derek Warwick in 1990 when his Lotus came flying out of the Parabolica upside down on the first lap. No sooner had his wheel-less wreck come to a stop than he popped his belts, ran back to the pits, got into the team's spare car and went out for the restart... Brave man!

HERO OF THE TRACK

Double World Champion Alberto Ascari was one of the greatest Italian drivers ever, and he made his mark at Monza. Not only did he win the Italian Grand Prix in 1951 and 1952 for Ferrari – going on to win the first of his two world titles in the second year – but he won the race in 1949, the year before the World Championship was created. It must be something in the blood, for his father, Antonio, also won the race in an Alfa Romeo way back in 1924.

INDIANAPOLIS

ROUND 15   SEPTEMBER 24, 2000

The Indianapolis Motor Speedway is one of the most famous racing circuits in the world, and few have such a rich racing lineage. And, in 2000, 'The Brickyard' is due to host a Grand Prix for the first time, albeit using little of its banking.

United States Grand Prix
I N D I A N A P O L I S

Circuit length: **TBC**
Race distance: **TBC**

24th

Timing sectors to be confirmed

NASCAR Circuit

'99 Pole: **TBC**
Winner: **TBC**

Indianapolis Motor Speedway, 2.610 miles/4.200km; 73 laps. Lap record: To be established for the Grand Prix circuit, but Arie Luyendyk holds the record for the original 2.5-mile banked oval circuit, with a lap of 37.895s set during the 1999 Indianapolis 500 that equates to a lap speed of 237.498mph

SOMETHING DIFFERENT: NASCAR Stock Cars have been a staple at Indianapolis Motor Speedway since the mid-'90s

America has always been a hugely important country for Formula One, especially since sponsorship became the backbone of the sport in the late 1960s. After all, which sponsor wouldn't be interested in exposure to the world's number one commercial market? Yet, they were disappointed as the United States Grand Prix was shunted around the country to increasingly unimpressive street circuits and attracted less and less interest. And then, in 1991, it finally dropped off the World Championship calendar. American motor sport fans, it seems, couldn't relate to Formula One's cosmopolitan image. It was too alien. What they wanted was their NASCAR stock cars, something they understood. And, after all, didn't the good ol' boys driving in NASCAR hit 230mph on the superspeedways, making them faster than the itty-bitty Formula One cars? So, for Formula One to hit back, it had to do so in a way that Americans understood, and where better to do that than to race on America's most famous circuit, the Indianapolis Motor Speedway?

Steeped in racing history

Opened in 1909, few tracks have been the scene for as much drama as the Indianapolis Motor Speedway, home of the annual 500-mile race, with close on 400,000 catered for in grandstands on three and a half sides of the 2.5-mile banked oval. Indianapolis has long been the domain of Indycars. Yet, in an attempt to give Formula One appeal in the USA, the Indianapolis 500 counted for World Championship points between 1950 and 1960, even though no Formula One cars or drivers took part and the Indycar drivers seldom competed in any Grands Prix, even their own United States Grand Prix. Ironically, just as the Indianapolis 500 was removed from the World Championship, so interest from Formula One grew, with Jack Brabham finishing ninth in 1961. Lotus made the biggest push, with their Formula One-derived racers darting in and out of the traditional front-engined Indycar roadsters as Jim Clark and Graham Hill won the race in 1965 and 1966 respectively. This changed the Indianapolis 500 forever as the locals opted to go the rear-engined route.

For those of you thinking of making a visit to this year's race there, this time of change is portrayed in the circuit's excellent museum.

However, the once invincible Indianapolis 500 – for years by far the most important sporting event on the American calendar – became a shadow of its former self once the circuit's owner Tony George formed the Indy Racing League in 1996 after falling out with the Indycar team owners. So, after a stand-off, the top teams went and raced in their own championship and he held on to the jewel in the Indycar crown, the Indianapolis 500. But he was the loser as the drivers in this were, to put it kindly, not from the top drawer. Indeed, George was forced to open the circuit to NASCAR stock cars for the Brickyard 400. Yet, for all the success of this race, the Indianapolis Motor Speedway was losing its prestige, which is the reason why he and Formula One impresario Bernie Ecclestone got together and masterminded a race that would do a world of good for both parties.

A tale of two straights

To describe a lap of the Indianapolis Motor Speedway is easy, as it consists only of two long straights linked by a pair of banked corners at either end. The circuit was even more tricky when opened in 1909 as it was made of crushed stone and many crashed fatally. This prompted owner Carl Fisher to pave the track instead, and he did so with more than three million bricks. Thus its nickname "The Brickyard". However, tarmac now covers all the circuit with the exception of a strip of bricks that mark the start/finish line.

But this is not the circuit on which the Formula One drivers will be plying their skills. Indeed, a special circuit has been built for the visitors, with only the start/finish straight and Turn One being used before the track peels off into the infield just before Turn Two. The track will then feed into a left-hand corner

CHASING THE DRAFT: The long, wide straights of the circuit's banked oval are perfect for slipstreaming. Only one straight will be used in the new Grand Prix track

followed by a sharp right and an even sharper left. A more open right pours the track onto the back straight which runs all the way along the back of the paddock to a right before a long left and a fast right.

A further right marks the far end of the circuit as this brings the track back to a right-left-right esse up onto the lightly banking main straight. If this infield section sounds worryingly twisty, don't worry as those who have seen it say that the track is unusually wide in order to make overtaking possible. That's one feature of racing that Americans insist upon, and quite right too…

HERO OF THE TRACK

Al Unser won the Indianapolis 500 four times, his brother Bobby won it twice and so did his son, Al Junior. So, you could say that the Unser family has a special place in the history of the Indianapolis Motor Speedway. And the Unser's success here puts the rival Andretti family in the shade, as Mario won the Indianapolis 500 only once and his son Michael never at all in careers that produced wins aplenty at all the other circuits visited by the Indycar championship.

SUZUKA

Japanese Grand Prix
S U Z U K A
Circuit length: **5.864km**
Race distance: **53 laps**

'S' Curves

Suzuka

Casio Triangle
Dunlop Curve

130R
Degner Curve

Hairpin

October
8th

Crossover

Spoon Curve

'99 Pole: **M Schumacher**
Winner: **Hakkinen**

Timing sectors

Suzuka, 3.644 miles/5.864km. 53
laps. Lap record: Heinz-Harald
Frentzen (Williams-Renault),
1m38.942s, 132.572mph, 1997

1999 results
1 Mika Hakkinen	McLaren
2 Michael Schumacher	Ferrari
3 Eddie Irvine	Ferrari
4 Heinz-Harald Frentzen	Jordan
5 Ralf Schumacher	Williams
6 Jean Alesi	Sauber

ROUND 16   OCTOBER 8, 2000

Suzuka may have been bumped from its traditional slot as the final race on Formula One's calendar, but it's sure to stage a dramatic race and will be enjoyed by the drivers as one of the best tracks.

Held as either the last or penultimate race of the season, the Japanese Grand Prix has seen more than its share of title shoot-outs. And last year's race at Suzuka may not have been as exciting as many of its predecessors, as Mika Hakkinen simply raced into a lead he wasn't to lose and thus collected the title. However, Suzuka will always be remembered for the scraps between Ayrton Senna and Alain Prost in 1989 and 1990.

By far the dominant drivers of the day, they collided on both occasions, with Prost becoming champion in 1989 as a result and Senna doing likewise the following year. Prior to last year's championship decider here, Damon Hill, Jacques Villeneuve and Hakkinen wrapped up titles at Suzuka in 1996, 1997 and 1998 respectively.

Hakkinen then made it two titles on the trot when he won at Suzuka

ACTION ASSURED: Fans who get a seat by Suzuka's Casio Triangle never fail to see some furious late-braking action

A TECHNICAL VENUE: Suzuka is a circuit that never lets the drivers relax. This is the climb out of the Dunlop Curves with the pits and paddock in the background

last year, but he had to fight for this honour, as he arrived here for the season's final race with a four-point deficit to Ferrari's Eddie Irvine. He knew that if he won and Irvine came second, then they'd be equal on points, but that he'd be champion with five wins to Irvine's four. So, a win was what he wanted. And a win was what he got, with Schumacher not doing enough to overhaul him and help team-mate Irvine who came home third.

A slow start

Japan took a long time to truly come around to Formula One. Certainly, you wouldn't have expected them to take part in the 1950s as they had no motor industry to talk of. By the 1960s, Honda had branched out from motorcycle racing to have a crack at Formula One, with some success. However, it wasn't until the late 1970s that Japan hosted a round of the World Championship for the first time. This was at Fuji Speedway at the foot of the sacred Mt Fuji volcano in 1976, when Mario Andretti splashed his Lotus through the rain to victory, Ferrari's Niki Lauda pulled off as he couldn't see in the spray and McLaren's James Hunt finished third to clinch the world title ahead of Lauda. A year later, Gilles Villeneuve's Ferrari hit Ronnie Peterson's Tyrrell and flipped over a fence, killing two people and putting a question mark over Fuji's suitability.

The Japanese Grand Prix was dropped until 1987 when it found its way back onto the calendar with a race at Suzuka, where it has remained to this day, resisting the claim from the TI Circuit that it should take over the slot. As it happens, the TI Circuit did get to hold a race under the guise of the Pacific Grand Prix in 1994 and 1995. However, Suzuka is the real stronghold of Japanese racing.

Every corner is tricky

Suzuka is a fast and very technical circuit on which to race, requiring endless testing for a driver to learn its many intricacies. Experience here counts, so all the Formula One drivers who spent a part of their careers racing in Japanese championships have a clear advantage, such as Eddie Irvine, Jacques Villeneuve, Heinz-Harald Frentzen, Mika Salo, Ralf Schumacher and, of course, the Japanese drivers.

From the grid, the track slopes down to the first corner, a double-apex right-hander out of which the drivers race uphill into a series of tricky esses, through which drivers can make up useful fractions of a second if they get it right. A fourth-gear left-hander is next, then on down to Degner Curve, a right-hander that takes the track under a bridge, through a kink into the left-hand hairpin. Then it's a curving, flat-out blast to Spoon curve. This is a long left-hander and it's crucial to get it right as it opens out on to the fastest section of the track. Halfway up the straight to the final chicane comes 130R, a sixth gear corner taken at around 155mph. The final corner is the ultra-tight chicane at which Gerhard Berger almost collected Damon Hill on the third lap of the 1996 Japanese Grand Prix. Then, kamikaze attacks avoided, the track bends right onto the start/finish straight.

The Suzuka circuit really is one of the classic tracks.

HERO OF THE TRACK

To this day, Aguri Suzuki gave Japanese Formula One fans their greatest moment when he climbed onto the Suzuka podium after the 1990 Japanese GP. And, what's more, he pulled off this feat driving a Larrousse, scarcely a fancied chassis... Still, it was a better car than the one he drove for the West team in 1989. Aguri went on to race for Footwork and Ligier, but never visited another podium. He is now a TV commentator and a promoter of young Japanese talent.

SEPANG

Malaysian Grand Prix
S E P A N G

Kuala Lumpar

Circuit length: **5.542km**
Race distance: **56 laps**

October
22nd

'99 Pole: **M Schumacher**
Winner: **Irvine**

0 = Turn number

Timing sectors

ROUND 17   OCTOBER 22, 2000

Sepang was a huge hit last year when it held a Grand Prix for the first time, with its fabulous facilities spoiled only by the soaring heat and humidity. But it's a more than welcome addition to the World Championship calendar.

Sepang, 3.444 miles/5.542km. 56 laps. Lap record: Michael Schumacher, 1m40.267s, 123.646mph, 1999

1999 results
1 Eddie Irvine	Ferrari
2 Michael Schumacher	Ferrari
3 Mika Hakkinen	McLaren
4 Johnny Herbert	Stewart
5 Rubens Barrichello	Stewart
6 Heinz-Harald Frentzen	Jordan

BEST SEATS IN THE HOUSE: The massive canopy provides welcome shade for those sitting in the huge grandstands

When people think back to the first ever Malaysian Grand Prix held last October, they will recall that this was the race in which Michael Schumacher made his comeback after a six-race lay-off with a broken leg and then controlled proceedings for Ferrari to allow Eddie Irvine to come through to win to add the maximum points score towards his World Championship challenge. However, they will also remember Schumacher driving a very wide and obstructive car in front of Mika Hakkinen's McLaren. Yet, most of all, they will remember the fact that the Ferraris were thrown out several hours after the race and that the outcome of the race was only decided a week later in a court room in Paris when Ferrari was handed its points back in an affair that left the sport seen

in a very bad light. Poor Hakkinen was even told he was World Champion for the second season running, only to have it taken away from him again in the courts. Fortunately, he kept a cool head and settled the matter beyond doubt in the Japanese Grand Prix.

However, this is all very unfair on the race organisers and the Malaysian government who had made a massive effort to ensure that its arrival on the Formula One calendar was a good one. And, indeed it was, with the circuit being extremely well received. All it needs for this year is a larger crowd, and this is likely to happen as Sepang has been awarded the final round of the championship rather than the penultimate, so a show-down is all but guaranteed...

INTO THE PITS: Michael Schumacher dives into the pits during a comeback run that saw him do everything that was humanly possible for Ferrari's championship cause

A meagre history

Malaysia has a meagre history of motorsport, having had races run only at temporary street circuits at Johore Batu and Penang before a permanent facility was built in 1968 near Kuala Lumpur. Known as Shah Alam, or sometimes as Selangor, this hosted a round of the Sportscar World Championship in 1985, but it was not a success and international racing slayed away.

With national racing series improving in the 1990s, hopes of a revival raised their head. South-East Asia then developed a motor racing network of its own in the 1990s, with its regional one-make single-seater category, Formula Asia, enjoying good growth, later to be replaced by the Asian Formula 2000 series. And the importance of having a cost-effective training formula has been proved by the development of Alex Yoong who graduated to the British Formula Three series in 1998 and then briefly to Formula 3000 last year.

Touring car racing remains the strongest draw in Malaysia, though, with the South-East Asian Touring Car Zone Challenge drawing in entries from Indonesia, Hong Kong and Thailand.

The plans for Malaysia to land a Grand Prix took a hit when a major downswing hit the South-East Asian economy and made this look extremely unlikely, as a greatly improved circuit would be needed as Shah Alam was too short, narrow and bumpy. However, those with the dream went ahead anyway and so Sepang was built near Kuala Lumpur in the ambitious Gateway Park complex that will also include bars, shops, restaurants and even an international airport eventually. And Sepang saw racing for the first time when a round of the Motorcycle World Championship was held there last April.

Pace-setting design

Smooth and wide, with a good mixture of corners and straights, the all-new Sepang circuit received the thumbs-up from all who saw it last year. It was even possible to overtake at some unlikely places, too, as David

Coulthard proved when he sprung a surprise move at the second corner and caught Michael Schumacher off guard.

Dominating the circuit's design is the 30,000-seater grandstand that runs not only alongside the start/finish straight, but doubles back on itself to look out over the second half of the lap and the approach to the final corner. The beauty of this huge edifice is that Sepang is built on level ground and thus the spectators can see as far as the predominantly slow and twisty corners spread on either side that connect these two straights.

A lap of Sepang commences with a dipping right-hand corner that is almost hairpin tight and is taken in second gear before feeding back into a left-hand hairpin, rather like a tightened-up version of the first two corners at the Hungaroring. The circuit then feeds off through a long right as the drivers change up through the gearbox onto a straight that ends with a tight right-hander. A longish left is followed by a more open, sixth gear right and a pair of fourth gear rights onto a short straight into a tight, left-hand hairpin.

From here, there are two more rights and a fifth gear left before a long right onto the back straight which takes the drivers up to another left-hand hairpin onto the start/finish straight, with this last corner a definite overtaking place. And if a driver fails to get by here, they could always have a go after tucking in behind the car in front down the start/finish straight into the first corner.

F1 REVIEW OF 1999

Anyone who witnessed the amazing speed of the McLarens in last year's opening race would have predicted that the season was going to be a McLaren walkover. But how wrong they proved to be as the 1999 Formula One season turned out to be one of the most open and keenly contested for years. And, while Mika Hakkinen was taken to the final round by a Ferrari driver it was by Eddie Irvine rather than the team's number one: Michael Schumacher.

When people look back at last season in the years to come, they will think that Mika Hakkinen just sneaked the World Championship title from Eddie Irvine, as he won by just two point. In some ways, they will be right, but in many others they will not have taken in the whole picture.

Although there was a McLaren versus Ferrari battle for honours, as there had been in 1998, it was an extremely unusual season. McLaren appeared to have the championship won after qualifying for the season's opening round in Melbourne, so great was their advantage over all the other cars on the grid. Indeed, they rocketed clear at the start. But then they broke. And this was to be a sign of the way that their season would run. Another sign was the identity of the Ferrari driver who then took the chequered flag, for it was Irvine, scoring his first Grand Prix win, while

Michael Schumacher had a troubled run and failed to score. Notable too was the fact that the minor podium places were filled by Heinz-Harald Frentzen for Jordan and Ralf Schumacher for Williams. These characters would all have important roles to play for the remaining 15 races of the campaign and would end the year filling the top six places in the championship.

McLaren showed next time out in Brazil that they had the pace to dominate, albeit not to the extent that they had shown in Australia. But, although Hakkinen took the garland, he'd suffered a minor mechanical problem while team-mate David Coulthard again failed to finish.

It soon became clear that McLaren was to miss out on a lot of points that should, by speed alone, have been theirs. And it was Ferrari's duo who were the recipients, as shown in the third round when Hakkinen

AUSTRALIAN GP BRAZILIAN GP SAN MARINO GP MONACO
AUSTRIAN GP GERMAN GP HUNGARIAN GP BELGIAN GP

THE JOY OF WINNING: Michael Schumacher shows just what it means to drivers to win a Grand Prix. He won two in 1999

crashed out of the lead at Imola – a feat he repeated four months later when dominating proceedings at Monza – allowing Schumacher through to win.

McLaren did appear to get its act together as Hakkinen led Coulthard home in Spain and then won again in Canada. But his car shed a wheel in the British Grand Prix, while Coulthard knocked him into a spin in Austria and then he suffered a blowout at Hockenheim, throwing away championship points by the handful.

It was at the British Grand Prix at Silverstone, though, that the identity of his championship title rival changed, as Michael Schumacher crashed and broke his right leg, putting him out for six races. Coulthard won on that day, but it could easily have been Irvine's win had he not overshot his pit. Then Irvine won both in Austria and in Germany as Hakkinen

stumbled and suddenly the Finn discovered that although Schumacher was off the scene, he still had a real threat from a driver from the Ferrari camp. Whereas Ferrari drafted in Mika Salo to act as a dutiful number two to Irvine, McLaren refused to force Coulthard into a subordinate role and it came mighty close to leaving Hakkinen short on points when the Scot led him home in the Belgian Grand Prix. However, it all worked out well for Hakkinen when he raced to victory in the final round at Suzuka to wrap up his second title on the trot. But it had been far more of a struggle than it ought to have been. Ferrari had to make do with winning the Constructors' Cup, something that it hadn't done since 1983.

Of the rest, Frentzen shone for Jordan, but Damon Hill didn't and so it was surprising that the team finished higher

than ever before, third overall. But Williams also had to make do with only one driver providing its points as Alessandro Zanardi failed to score at all, something that left the way clear for Stewart to pip them to fourth overall in a year in which the team scored its first ever win, which it was desperate to do before metamorphosing into Jaguar Racing for the coming season. Williams is not accustomed to finishing this low, and will be hoping that its new link with BMW will bear fruit soon.

Having the right engine is vital to success in Formula One, though, and British American Racing will be hoping that its new deal for works Honda engines will help it score its first points, wins even, after a wretched debut season in which it failed to achieve either of these aims that it seemed to have said would be its own as though by divine right.

GP SPANISH GP CANADIAN GP FRENCH GP BRITISH GP
ITALIAN GP EUROPEAN GP MALAYSIAN GP JAPANESE GP

F1

THE YEAR IN PICTURES

AUSTRALIAN GP

EDDIE THE FIRST

RACE RESULTS

ROUND 1 AT MELBOURNE, MARCH 7, 1999

57 LAPS—187.81 MILES

	Driver	Team
1	EDDIE IRVINE	Ferrari
2	HEINZ-HARALD FRENTZEN	Jordan
3	RALF SCHUMACHER	Williams
4	GIANCARLO FISICHELLA	Benetton
5	RUBENS BARRICHELLO	Stewart
6	PEDRO DE LA ROSA	Arrows

POLE Hakkinen, 1m 30.462s (131.13mph/211.02kph)
FASTEST LAP M Schumacher, 1m 32.112s (128.78mph/207.25kph)
WEATHER Warm, dry and bright

Ferrari won the season-opener as McLaren flopped at Melbourne. However, it wasn't Michael Schumacher who took the chequered flag, but team-mate Eddie Irvine for the very first time.

There were three things that you need to know about this race. First off, the McLarens should have won it easily, but both failed. Secondly, Michael Schumacher and fellow second row qualifier Rubens Barrichello both started from the back of the grid. Thirdly, Eddie Irvine was there to pick up the pieces, as he would do again before the year was over. Unwittingly, this summed up the season ahead: McLaren fallibility; disappointment for Michael Schumacher; promise and disappointment for Barrichello; and speed and opportunism from Irvine.

The pitlane was rocked by the speed of the McLarens in qualifying, with third-ranked Schumacher 1.3 seconds off Hakkinen's time. The start was aborted as both Stewarts were smoking on the grid. With their wiring looms burned, both cars were out for the day. But the re-start meant that Barrichello would be able to start from the pitlane, while Herbert was confined to spectating.

Then Schumacher failed to get away on the parade lap for the re-start and so had to begin from the back. The McLarens were already 10 seconds clear of Irvine by the sixth lap, but it was a case of unlucky lap 13 for Coulthard as he parked up in the garage, his car stuck in sixth gear. Hakkinen lasted little longer, retiring on lap 22 with a throttle linkage problem.

However, two important events had happened in the interim. Firstly, Jacques Villeneuve marked the British American Racing team's debut with a huge accident that brought out the safety car. Then, running behind this safety car, Hakkinen discovered that he wasn't getting the expected throttle response and this caught out the cars behind when they were released as the safety car withdrew to the pitlane, as everyone braked not to pass him as the yellow flags were still out. Lying eighth in the queue after strong early progress, Barrichello braked hard but still nosed past Schumacher and earned himself a stop-go penalty…

With the McLarens gone, Irvine was out front and remained clear of challenges from Heinz-Harald Frentzen's Jordan and Ralf Schumacher's Williams to score his first win at the 82nd time of trying. Giancarlo Fisichella was a distant fourth for Benetton, with Barrichello frustrated by his extra stop leaving him fifth. Still, at least he scored, unlike Michael Schumacher who fell to eighth and last after a puncture cost him time.

NICE ONE EDDIE: Arm aloft, Eddie Irvine opens his 1999 championship campaign with his first Grand Prix victory

AUSTRALIAN GP

EDDIE THE FIRST

Ferrari won the season-opener as McLaren flopped at Melbourne. However, it wasn't Michael Schumacher who took the chequered flag, but team-mate Eddie Irvine for the very first time.

RACE RESULTS

**ROUND 1 AT MELBOURNE,
MARCH 7, 1999**

57 LAPS—187.81 MILES

Driver	Team
1 EDDIE IRVINE	Ferrari
2 HEINZ-HARALD FRENTZEN	Jordan
3 RALF SCHUMACHER	Williams
4 GIANCARLO FISICHELLA	Benetton
5 RUBENS BARRICHELLO	Stewart
6 PEDRO DE LA ROSA	Arrows

POLE Hakkinen, 1m 30.462s
(131.13mph/211.02kph)
FASTEST LAP M Schumacher,
1m 32.112s (128.78mph/207.25kph)
WEATHER Warm, dry and bright

There were three things that you need to know about this race. First off, the McLarens should have won it easily, but both failed. Secondly, Michael Schumacher and fellow second row qualifier Rubens Barrichello both started from the back of the grid. Thirdly, Eddie Irvine was there to pick up the pieces, as he would do again before the year was over. Unwittingly, this summed up the season ahead: McLaren fallibility; disappointment for Michael Schumacher; promise and disappointment for Barrichello; and speed and opportunism from Irvine.

The pitlane was rocked by the speed of the McLarens in qualifying, with third-ranked Schumacher 1.3 seconds off Hakkinen's time. The start was aborted as both Stewarts were smoking on the grid. With their wiring looms burned, both cars were out for the day. But the re-start meant that Barrichello would be able to start from the pitlane, while Herbert was confined to spectating.

Then Schumacher failed to get away on the parade lap for the re-start and so had to begin from the back. The McLarens were already 10 seconds clear of Irvine by the sixth lap, but it was a case of unlucky lap 13 for Coulthard as he parked up in the garage, his car stuck in sixth gear. Hakkinen lasted little longer, retiring on lap 22 with a throttle linkage problem.

However, two important events had happened in the interim. Firstly, Jacques Villeneuve marked the British American Racing team's debut with a huge accident that brought out the safety car. Then, running behind this safety car, Hakkinen discovered that he wasn't getting the expected throttle response and this caught out the cars behind when they were released as the safety car withdrew to the pitlane, as everyone braked not to pass him as the yellow flags were still out. Lying eighth in the queue after strong early progress, Barrichello braked hard but still nosed past Schumacher and earned himself a stop-go penalty…

With the McLarens gone, Irvine was out front and remained clear of challenges from Heinz-Harald Frentzen's Jordan and Ralf Schumacher's Williams to score his first win at the 82nd time of trying. Giancarlo Fisichella was a distant fourth for Benetton, with Barrichello frustrated by his extra stop leaving him fifth. Still, at least he scored, unlike Michael Schumacher who fell to eighth and last after a puncture cost him time.

NICE ONE EDDIE: Arm aloft, Eddie Irvine opens his 1999 championship campaign with his first Grand Prix victory

BRAZILIAN GP

RACE RESULTS
ROUND 2 AT INTERLAGOS, APRIL 11, 1999
72 LAPS—192.02 MILES

	Driver	Team
1	MIKA HAKKINEN	McLaren
2	MICHAEL SCHUMACHER	Ferrari
3	HEINZ-HARALD FRENTZEN	Jordan
4	RALF SCHUMACHER	Williams
5	EDDIE IRVINE	Ferrari
6	OLIVIER PANIS	Prost

POLE Hakkinen, 1m 16.568s
(125.39mph/201.79kph)
FASTEST LAP Hakkinen, 1m 18.448s
(123.63mph/198.95kph)
WEATHER Hot, dry and sunny

RUBENS LEADS, MIKA WINS

Gearbox problems were apparent at McLaren again and offered Rubens Barrichello the chance to lead. Michael Schumacher got by too, but Mika Hakkinen was ahead by the finish.

McLaren had dominated at Interlagos in 1998, when only Ferrari's Michael Schumacher managed to finish on the same lap. And, after qualifying, it looked as though it was going to be a case of more of the same, with Hakkinen on pole and David Coulthard alongside. Barrichello was next up for the blossoming Stewart team, but he was three-quarters of a second away from pole. Importantly, though, he was ahead of Melbourne sparring partner Michael Schumacher who was rattled by the speed of the McLarens and criticized Ferrari for the first time since joining them in 1996.

The red lights came on, they went out and Hakkinen powered into the lead. Coulthard didn't go with him, though, stalling on the grid. He got away, but was last and parked up after 22 laps.

Then Hakkinen suddenly slowed on the fourth lap and Barrichello rocketed into the lead, sending the home crowd wild. Schumacher went past too as the Finn pulled to the side of the track. But then he got going again. Fifth gear had gone missing, but the team told Mika to try and continue and fortunately the gears came back.

Hakkinen then sat on Schumacher's tail, clearly faster, but unable to get by. They moved into first and second when Barrichello revealed what people suspected: he was going to be two-stopping while Schumacher and Hakkinen planned just one stop apiece. It counted for nothing, though, as Rubens retired with engine failure. All that was left was for Mika to overtake Michael when he put in four quick laps after the Ferrari driver pitted, before making his own stop. And that was that, with Michael trailing him home a dispirited second, knowing that he only got close because of Mika's gearbox problems.

HOME-TOWN HERO: Rubens Barrichello set the crowds whooping when he led

Heinz-Harald Frentzen was a distant third, a place he inherited when Eddie Irvine had to make an extra stop to have a pneumatic problem seen to, also falling behind Ralf Schumacher's Williams.

Ricardo Zonta was deprived of the chance to show his skills to his home crowd as he shunted heavily in testing and would be out for four races. Minardi, on the other hand, had already amended its line-up, with Formula 3000 hotshot Stephane Sarrazin standing in for Luca Badoer who had broken a hand several weeks earlier.

SAN MARINO GP

HAKKINEN TRIPS UP

Tactical superiority from Ferrari's Ross Brawn and a mistake from Mika Hakkinen when leading gave Michael Schumacher the win he so wanted in front of the *tifosi* at Imola.

Mika Hakkinen could have had no idea when he motored onto the 17th lap of the San Marino GP with a lead of a dozen seconds and under no pressure that he was about to make a mistake that would not only cost him the race, but prove to be the first of a two-part Italian farce.

The front row of the grid was all-McLaren yet again, but the Ferraris were considerably closer, with Michael Schumacher less than a fifth of a second away from pole. However, come the race, Hakkinen powered away by almost a second a lap from team-mate David Coulthard, making it clear that he was running a two-stop strategy and the Scot looking to stop just the once.

And so the pattern was set, but then, coming through Traguardo onto the start/finish straight, Mika rode a fraction too far over the kerbs as he endeavoured to press home his advantage. The silver car snapped left and slammed into the barriers right in front of all the people on the pit-wall. But even worse, right in front of the *tifosi*, this vociferous bunch erupting as they realized that they hadn't been imagining it.

However, there was still the small matter of Coulthard between them and their dreams, the Scot inheriting the lead as Mika clambered sheepishly out of his broken car. With Imola notoriously difficult for overtaking, Ferrari had to think fast. Yet again, master tactician Ross Brawn called it right, bringing Michael in on lap 31. Coulthard came in four laps later and failed to emerge still in the lead. So, job done, and that was how it stayed to the finish, with Coulthard later slamming Olivier Panis for blocking him after his pitstop.

Rubens Barrichello was a whole lap in arrears in third place – a whole lap down, but just a second ahead of Damon Hill's Jordan. The gap was made this large when Eddie Irvine dropped out with a blown engine and Heinz-Harald Frentzen, next up, spun off on the resultant slick… Amazingly, the same thing happened with four laps to go as Johnny Herbert's engine blew and as he pulled off from fifth place, Alessandro Zanardi lost a points-drive as he too slid off on the oil.

SUCCESS AND FAILURE: Michael Schumacher shows his delight at winning, while Coulthard's demeanour reveals what he thought of second

MONACO GP

ADVANTAGE SCHUMACHER

This may have been Ferrari's second win of the year, but this one was achieved in a straight fight with McLaren. No wonder Michael Schumacher was utterly delighted.

RACE RESULTS

ROUND 4 AT MONACO, MAY 16, 1999

78 LAPS—163.18 MILES

	Driver	Team
1	MICHAEL SCHUMACHER	Ferrari
2	EDDIE IRVINE	Ferrari
3	MIKA HAKKINEN	McLaren
4	HEINZ-HARALD FRENTZEN	Jordan
5	GIANCARLO FISICHELLA	Benetton
6	ALEXANDER WURZ	Benetton

POLE Hakkinen, 1m 20.547s
(93.50mph/150.47kph)
FASTEST LAP Hakkinen, 1m 22.259s
(91.56mph/147.35kph)
WEATHER Warm, dry and sunny

FERRARI POWER: Michael Schumacher gets the jump on Hakkinen, while Irvine does likewise to Coulthard behind

Three races gone and the McLaren drivers found themselves in the alien position of not being at the top of the timesheets in qualifying. No matter what they did, Michael Schumacher sat on provisional pole position. Or he did until the dying minutes of the one-hour session, when Mika Hakkinen threaded together a lap that knocked the German back to second place by just 0.064 seconds.

With few circuits offering as little in the way of overtaking opportunities, this was a massive blow to Michael. However, he did the only thing he could do when the five red lights were extinguished at the start, blasting from the pitwall side of the grid, and nosing in front of Hakkinen

before the first corner, Ste Devote. To compound McLaren's woe, Eddie Irvine did likewise to move past David Coulthard into third.

Immediately, people suspected that Ferrari had sent its cars out with a lighter fuel load as they would be two-stopping. But, with passing so difficult, this is not a tactic people would choose for Monaco. So, they guessed again that the Ferrari drivers were simply planning to make their one stop earlier than the McLaren duo.

Schumacher eased away from Hakkinen, who soon found that his car's handling had gone awry. But this counted for little later on, as the most damage was done when he hit oil and lost almost 20 seconds after sliding up an

escape road in one of the few moments of excitement in a dull race. Schumacher was clear and went away to his second win on the trot.

Adding to Ferrari's delight, Irvine grabbed second place, with Hakkinen's slip saving him from having to overtake him after his second stop. Coulthard ran fourth until his gearbox failed again, and so Heinz-Harald Frentzen took his third helping of good points in four races, easily clear of the Benettons of Giancarlo Fisichella and Alexander Wurz, both of whom were elevated when Rubens Barrichello's suspension collapsed with half-a-dozen laps to run, just as team-mate Johnny Herbert's had earlier in the race.

SPANISH GP

MCLAREN SHOWS WHO IS BOSS

This was the result that people had expected ever since the opening race, a McLaren one-two, with Mika Hakkinen first and David Coulthard second. But it didn't make for exciting viewing.

RACE RESULTS

ROUND 5 AT BARCELONA,
MAY 30, 1999

65 LAPS—190.97 MILES

	Driver	Team
1	MIKA HAKKINEN	McLaren
2	DAVID COULTHARD	McLaren
3	MICHAEL SCHUMACHER	Ferrari
4	EDDIE IRVINE	Ferrari
5	RALF SCHUMACHER	Williams
6	JARNO TRULLI	Prost

POLE Hakkinen, 1m 22.088s
(128.85mph/207.35kph)
FASTEST LAP Michael Schumacher,
1m 24.982s (124.45mph/200.28kph)
WEATHER Hot, dry and sunny

BACK ON TRACK: Mika Hakkinen raced to his second win of 1999 in Spain following his troubled start to his World Championship title defence

McLaren had controlled proceedings at Barcelona's Circuit de Catalunya in 1998. And 1999 was clearly going to be no different as Hakkinen grabbed his fifth pole of the year, from five attempts... However, Coulthard lined up behind him rather than alongside. Yes, there was a Ferrari on the front row, something of a surprise on a circuit that appeared almost tailor-made for McLaren's design. But there was a further shock – the Ferrari on the inside of the front row was that of Eddie Irvine, not Michael Schumacher. And his time was just over a tenth of a second slower than Hakkinen's, with both Coulthard and Schumacher within a tenth of his time. However, the situation had been made artificially close by the fact that the Ferraris had gone out on Bridgestone's softer tyres and would thus have to use these in the race.

Ferrari's best hope was thus to get the jump on the McLarens at the start, as they had at Monaco, and then control the race from the front. However, the reverse happened as Hakkinen led away from Coulthard. Schumacher held position, with Irvine falling to fifth and both being headed by Jacques Villeneuve's BAR, up from sixth on the grid. Having got into a good position for the first time for BAR, the Canadian guarded his rear. And this was how it stayed to the first pitstops, with the McLaren duo easing away.

On a circuit on which overtaking appears nigh on impossible, there were no changes for the top placings until the Ferraris made their first stops before Villeneuve did and were both ahead by the time he re-emerged. Villeneuve's day went downhill from there as his car suffered transmission failure as he tried to pull away from his second stop.

Schumacher drove a startling second stint to catch Coulthard, but then came the second round of stops and the Scot stayed ahead to the finish as the top-four held position. Ralf Schumacher was the last runner on the lead lap, in fifth. While the battle for sixth was one of the few points of excitement in the race, with Jarno Trulli, Rubens Barrichello and Damon Hill having a great tussle. This was not what Hakkinen wanted to find when he came around to lap them. But he was able to get through with his lead intact.

CANADIAN GP

MICHAEL SLIPS UP

Mika Hakkinen threw away the lead by crashing at Imola. At Montreal, it was Michael Schumacher's turn to return the favour and Hakkinen came away with a welcome victory.

RACE RESULTS

ROUND 6 AT MONTREAL,
JUNE 13, 1999

69 LAPS—189.55 MILES

Driver	Team
1 MIKA HAKKINEN	McLaren
2 GIANCARLO FISICHELLA	Benetton
3 EDDIE IRVINE	Ferrari
4 RALF SCHUMACHER	Williams
5 JOHNNY HERBERT	Stewart
6 PEDRO DINIZ	Sauber

POLE M Schumacher, 1m 19.298s
(124.71mph/200.69kph)
FASTEST LAP Irvine, 1m 20.382s
(123.03mph/197.99kph)
WEATHER Hot, dry and sunny

I f the Spanish Grand Prix had made pundits the world over say that something had to be done to make Formula One more exciting, the Canadian Grand Prix proved that there was life in the old dog yet. For the second year running,

the race in Montreal turned out to be a belter.

Michael Schumacher set the ball rolling by claiming pole position for Ferrari ahead of Mika Hakkinen. All the more impressively, he set his time on his first run and then waited in the pits

A HAPPY FINN: Mika Hakkinen shows how it feels to lead the championship

for anyone to beat it. And they couldn't.

Michael then made a good start and led into the first corner, with Hakkinen, Eddie Irvine, Giancarlo Fisichella and David Coulthard tucking in behind. However, as in 1998, there was trouble in the pack at the tight left first corner and, again as in 1998, Jarno Trulli made contact with Jean Alesi. He hit Rubens Barrichello too, even taking a chunk out of the Brazilian's helmet.

The safety car came out while this was cleared up, but when it released the remaining cars to race again Coulthard rocketed past Fisichella for fourth place. He hardly had time to enjoy his promotion before the safety car was out again, this time after Ricardo Zonta had slammed his BAR into the wall at Turn 15, the left-handed part of the esses onto the start/finish straight. He was to find himself in good company, as Damon Hill did likewise on lap 15, then Michael Schumacher did the same from the lead on lap 30 and Jacques Villeneuve became the third former World Champion to do so at the same point on lap 35…

Michael Schumacher was contrite, explaining that he had been doing his all to build a margin over Hakkinen. It was uncannily like what happened in Imola, only in reverse. Hakkinen was left in a lead he wasn't to lose, but behind him Coulthard and Irvine clashed shortly after the third safety car period. Irvine dropped to eighth but kept going, while Coulthard pitted for a check-up and waved goodbye to any points.

Irvine was on a mission and was up to fourth with four laps to go when Heinz-Harald Frentzen crashed his Jordan heavily out of second and left Fisichella as runner-up. With the safety car out again and staying out until the finish, Irvine had to make do with third.

FRENCH GP

FRENTZEN IS THE RAIN MAN

RACE RESULTS

ROUND 7 AT MAGNY-COURS, JUNE 27, 1999

72 LAPS—190.02 MILES

Driver	Team
1 HEINZ-HARALD FRENTZEN	Jordan
2 MIKA HAKKINEN	McLaren
3 RUBENS BARRICHELLO	Stewart
4 RALF SCHUMACHER	Williams
5 MICHAEL SCHUMACHER	Ferrari
6 EDDIE IRVINE	Ferrari

POLE Barrichello, 1m 38.441s (96.58mph/155.43kph)
FASTEST LAP Coulthard, 1m 19.227s (120.00mph/193.11kph)
WEATHER Cool, very wet and heavy rain

There has seldom been a Grand Prix with weather like it. Rain, rain and more rain. However, through it all came Heinz-Harald Frentzen to give Jordan its second victory.

Magny-Cours was awash in June. The meeting started with light rain for the untimed sessions on the Friday morning and became progressively wetter through to the finish.

So, with aquaplaning the most common driver complaint, qualifying was a lottery. It was the brave who were rewarded – those who decided to go for it and set a quick time early on, just in case conditions actually got worse, which they did. As happened at the 1994 Belgian Grand Prix, it was Rubens Barrichello who got it right, this time to give Stewart its first pole. Jean Alesi and Olivier Panis also set their times early and ended up second and third for Sauber and Prost. But perhaps the drive of qualifying came from David Coulthard who set the fourth fastest time when conditions were worse later on. Michael Schumacher qualified sixth, while Mika Hakkinen was 14th and Eddie Irvine 17th. The Ulsterman was just the right side of the 107 per cent cut-off point. Damon Hill was just the wrong side, but the rule of *force majeure* was rightly used and all 22 cars were allowed to start.

It was dry at the start of the race and Barrichello led until lap 6 when Coulthard shot past. He then rocketed clear before his alternator failed. Hakkinen wasn't hanging about either, and was up to second (from 14th!) by lap 19, three places ahead of Michael Schumacher.

Hakkinen took the lead just before the first round of stops, which is when it started to rain. Stewart proved faster than McLaren in the pits, and Barrichello re-emerged just in front.

Five minutes later, the circuit was awash, with Alesi skating out of third and many others spinning. The safety car came out and that almost spun too. Once the rivers had stopped running quite so deep across the track, racing resumed and Hakkinen took a run at Barrichello into the hairpin and spun, falling to seventh. This elevated Michael Schumacher to second, and he soon found himself in the lead. But he was having gearchange problems and pitted for a new steering wheel. Barrichello was leading again, this time from Frentzen. Hakkinen passed them both but he and Barrichello needed to pit once more, while Frentzen had done just enough to stretch his fuel to the end of the race for his second win, and his first for Jordan.

CHANGING ORDER: Heinz-Harald Frentzen proved to be top German on the day, winning ahead of the Schumachers

BRITISH GP

SCHUMACHER'S BAD BREAK

This was the race for the number twos as David Coulthard and Eddie Irvine finished first and second, while Mika Hakkinen lost a wheel and Michael Schumacher fractured a leg.

RACE RESULTS

F1

ROUND 8 AT SILVERSTONE,
JULY 11, 1999

60 LAPS—191.53 MILES

Driver	Team
1 DAVID COULTHARD	McLaren
2 EDDIE IRVINE	Ferrari
3 RALF SCHUMACHER	Williams
4 HEINZ-HARALD FRENTZEN	Jordan
5 DAMON HILL	Jordan
6 PEDRO DINIZ	Sauber

POLE Hakkinen, 1m 24.804s
(135.31mph/217.75kph)
FASTEST LAP Hakkinen, 1m 26.788s
(132.49mph/213.21kph)
WEATHER Hot, dry and sunny

The main talking point between the teams dripping away from the French Grand Prix and arriving at Silverstone was whether Damon Hill had decided to alter his decision to retire at the end of the season and call it a day immediately after his lacklustre drive in France. After much soul-searching, Damon had decided to race on, but perhaps only for this race.

However, this was batted out of the headlines moments after the race was stopped as Jacques Villeneuve and Alessandro Zanardi had stalled and were stationary on the grid. The drivers at the front of the field acknowledged the red flags as they powered down the Hangar Straight, Mika Hakkinen heading David Coulthard and Eddie Irvine. Seemingly as though he had been too busy trying to get past Irvine, Michael Schumacher lunged past his team-mate into Stowe, then bounded through the gravel trap and hard into the tyrewall. It transpired that Michael had not been trying anything, but that his rear brakes had failed, and the outcome of the heavy impact was that he'd broken his right leg in two places.

The race was re-started and looked to be a Hakkinen benefit as he stretched his advantage over Irvine and Coulthard, with Heinz-Harald Frentzen an increasingly distant fourth. But then there was trouble changing the Finn's right rear wheel. No sooner had he left the pitlane than it was clear that it was loose and he was forced to stop again. His second stop took an age, but it actually helped the team as his crew was working on the problem when Irvine came in for his first stop at the adjacent pit and overshot. It cost him around five seconds and meant that Coulthard was narrowly ahead as he rejoined.

Already out of the reckoning, Hakkinen then lost the troublesome wheel just as he

GOING FOR THE GAP: Frentzen tries to dive between Coulthard and Irvine

approached the pit entry. He dived in on three wheels, took on a fourth wheel and rejoined, but was soon withdrawn on safety grounds.

This left Coulthard to race to a much-needed victory ahead of Irvine and Ralf Schumacher, the German having driven courageously since he could not be sure of the full extent of his brother's injuries. He was made to work for his points, though, as Frentzen was all over his tail in the closing laps.

AUSTRIAN GP

NUMBER TWO BECOMES NUMBER ONE

Ferrari without Michael Schumacher was not expected to come away from Austria with victory, but they received more than a little help from McLaren's men on the opening lap...

RACE RESULTS
ROUND 9 AT A1-RING, JULY 25, 1999

71 LAPS—190.54 MILES

	Driver	Team
1	EDDIE IRVINE	Ferrari
2	DAVID COULTHARD	McLaren
3	MIKA HAKKINEN	McLaren
4	HEINZ-HARALD FRENTZEN	Jordan
5	ALEXANDER WURZ	Benetton
6	PEDRO DINIZ	Sauber

POLE Hakkinen, 1m 10.954s
(136.18mph/219.15kph)
FASTEST LAP Hakkinen, 1m 12.107s
(133.99mph/215.62kph)
WEATHER Warm, dry and bright

INTERNECINE STRIFE: Hakkinen wonders what's going on after being spun on the opening lap by his own team-mate

Imagine the scene. Ferrari arrived at the A1-Ring without the one ingredient around which all other factors had been arranged since the start of 1996. There was no Michael Schumacher, for he was at home in Switzerland, convalescing. And the train of thought was that without the German, they had no chance of beating the McLarens. This appeared to be the case after qualifying, as although Eddie Irvine was third, he was a second away from Mika Hakkinen's pole time, on a track with a short lap.

Then a miracle happened. The field streamed through the tight first corner without trouble. But Hakkinen left the door open at the equally tight second corner and David Coulthard couldn't resist having a go. No sooner had he dived for it than it was clear that the Finn hadn't

considered that his team-mate would try such a thing and started swinging across to the apex. It was too late for Coulthard to avoid him and he spun the Finn around. The field bunched behind and Ferrari stand-in Mika Salo damaged his car's nose as Hakkinen had to sit waiting for the field to pass before spinning himself back into the race. Coulthard, no doubt rattled by what he'd just done, then led from Rubens Barrichello and Irvine. This was how they stayed to their only planned pit-stops, while Hakkinen carved his way up from last. By mid-distance, he was up to fourth.

Barrichello was the first of the leading trio to pit, then Coulthard, then, five laps later, Irvine. Such had been Irvine's pace in those crucial laps that he emerged in the lead.

Infuriated by this, Coulthard closed right in, especially in the closing laps when Irvine's brakes were all but finished, but he just couldn't find a way past.

Hakkinen motored on to third place, but he certainly didn't shake Coulthard's hand on the podium afterwards… While Barrichello lost fourth place when his engine failed, elevating Heinz-Harald Frentzen to yet another useful batch of points.

It had been another piece of tactical mastery from Ferrari, but it proved that Irvine could also press on when asked, just like Michael Schumacher. So, perhaps Ferrari wasn't out of the title race after all. It led the Constructors' Cup by two points, with Irvine a similar margin behind Hakkinen.

GERMAN GP

FERRARI'S DOUBLE TOP

Ferrari scored a major coup by finishing one-two ahead of McLaren on Mercedes' home patch. Mika Hakkinen, though, was simply happy to be alive after a 200mph blow-out.

RACE RESULTS

ROUND 10 AT HOCKENHEIM, AUGUST 1, 1999

45 LAPS—190.78 MILES

	Driver	Team
1	EDDIE IRVINE	Ferrari
2	MIKA SALO	Ferrari
3	HEINZ-HARALD FRENTZEN	Jordan
4	RALF SCHUMACHER	Williams
5	DAVID COULTHARD	McLaren
6	JARNO TRULLI	Prost

POLE Hakkinen, 1m 42.950s (148.27mph/238.60kph)
FASTEST LAP Coulthard, 1m 45.270s (144.99mph/233.28kph)
WEATHER Hot, dry and sunny

Few circuits were thought to suit the McLaren MP4-14s better than this one, with the long straights ideal for the Mercedes engines to exercise their wealth of horsepower. However, Heinz-Harald Frentzen showed that the Mugen Honda in his Jordan also packed a punch and set provisional pole position in qualifying. Mika Hakkinen beat it to record his eighth pole of the year, but only just. David Coulthard started third, but in the back of his mind must have lurked the spectre of one of his rear tyres throwing its tread at 200mph during practice. Johnny Herbert had also experienced a fright, as he had his rear wing fail approaching the Ostkurve chicane. The Ferraris were fourth and fifth, albeit with Mika Salo ahead of Eddie Irvine.

The race looked to be a formality for Hakkinen after he made a strong start, but Coulthard was going to have to work a little harder as he had been beaten to the first corner by Salo, while Frentzen fell to fourth. On lap three, Rubens Barrichello used his Stewart's ample Ford horsepower to demote the German to fifth, having passed Irvine at the start. However, a hydraulic failure saw the Brazilian on the sidelines within a few laps.

Not everyone made it away from the start, though, with Jacques Villeneuve recording his tenth straight retirement for BAR when he was tipped into Pedro Diniz on the run to the first corner, with both drivers crashing out.

Coulthard ducked and dived in an attempt to find a way around Salo, but clipped the Ferrari at the Ostkurve chicane on lap 10 and had to pit for a new nose, re-emerging in tenth place.

Hakkinen's one planned pitstop went awry, with his refuelling rig failing and the crew having to swap over to Coulthard's. Hakkinen fell to fourth. He passed Frentzen for third then immediately had a blow-out approaching the stadium at 200mph and spun into the tyrewall at the Agip Kurve after slowing through a gravel trap. Luckily, he stepped out unharmed.

Now the race was Ferrari's, with Salo leading for a lap before Irvine came onto his tail and he waved him through. They went on to finish first and second, to give Irvine an eight-point championship lead, so no wonder that he felt moved to hand his winner's trophy to Salo afterwards. Frentzen finished third, ahead of Ralf Schumacher and a frustrated Coulthard who had lost further ground with a 10 second stop-go penalty for cutting a chicane.

PURE DELIGHT: Eddie Irvine lets rip with the bubbly after being handed victory by his stand-in team-mate Mika Salo, to whom he gave the trophy

HUNGARIAN GP

MCLAREN GETS IT RIGHT

McLaren really needed a race with no mistakes to put itself back on track, and this was duly delivered as Mika Hakkinen and David Coulthard claimed a controlled one-two.

RACE RESULTS

ROUND 11 AT HUNGARORING, AUGUST 15, 1999

77 LAPS—190.04 MILES

	Driver	Team
1	MIKA HAKKINEN	McLaren
2	DAVID COULTHARD	McLaren
3	EDDIE IRVINE	Ferrari
4	HEINZ-HARALD FRENTZEN	Jordan
5	RUBENS BARRICHELLO	Stewart
6	DAMON HILL	Jordan

POLE Hakkinen, 1m 18.156s
(113.68mph/182.94kph)
FASTEST LAP Coulthard, 1m 20.699s
(110.13mph/177.23kph)
WEATHER Warm, dry and sunny

There's no circuit like the Hungaroring for offering drivers little prospect of overtaking. Put simply, a driver will almost never find his way past the driver ahead unless the one in front makes a mistake. And while that may make for close racing, it doesn't make for exciting racing. So, no wonder Ferrari pulled off a coup in 1998 when it used a three-stop strategy to guide Michael Schumacher past the two McLarens that were running ahead of him.

The business of securing that coveted pole position was therefore even more serious than ever, and it duly went to Mika Hakkinen. But Eddie Irvine had worked wonders to place his Ferrari alongside him, with David Coulthard third. Irvine, though, couldn't look to his teammate for support, as Mika Salo could not get a feel for his Ferrari chassis around this unusually twisty track and lined up in 18th place.

After a run of disappointments, all Hakkinen wanted was a trouble-free race, and he cleared the first hurdle by leading to the first corner. It had been hoped that Coulthard would be able to grab second as Irvine was starting on the dirty side of the grid. But quite the reverse happened as he went backwards instead, falling to fifth behind Giancarlo Fisichella and Heinz-Harald Frentzen.

However, by running a long first stint before his first stop, Coulthard was able to climb to third ahead of this pair. Rubens Barrichello stayed out even longer as he was running a one-stop strategy, and rose to third, but this saw him fall to eighth when he came back out.

With Hakkinen driving impeccably to open out a comfortable lead, Coulthard got his head down and caught Irvine. They both dived in to their second stop at the same time, but Irvine just squeezed out ahead. However, the McLaren was clearly faster and on lap 63 Irvine pressed a shade too hard and spun, letting Coulthard through to third. And that was how they finished, with Frentzen fourth, Barrichello fifth and Damon Hill sixth. Yes, he hadn't hung up his helmet and had elected to stay on until he knew that Jordan was safe in third place in the Constructors' Cup.

JOB DONE: The McLarens are parked up in *parc ferme* after their one-two

BELGIAN GP

RACE RESULTS
ROUND 12 AT SPA-FRANCORCHAMPS, AUGUST 29, 1999

44 LAPS—190.52 MILES

F1

REVIEW OF THE
1999 SEASON

115

Driver	Team
1 DAVID COULTHARD	McLaren
2 MIKA HAKKINEN	McLaren
3 HEINZ-HARALD FRENTZEN	Jordan
4 EDDIE IRVINE	Ferrari
5 RALF SCHUMACHER	Williams
6 DAMON HILL	Jordan

POLE Hakkinen, 1m 50.329s
(141.29mph/227.37kph)
FASTEST LAP Hakkinen, 1m 53.955s
(136.78mph/220.12kph)
WEATHER Warm, dry and sunny

DAVID BEATS GOLIATH

McLaren continued to pride itself on having no team orders, but Mika Hakkinen was not at all happy after losing valuable championship points by being beaten to victory by David Coulthard.

Michael Schumacher raised Ferrari's hopes in the week after the Hungarian Grand Prix when he had a successful test at Mugello, lapping as fast as Eddie Irvine. But he suffered pain when cycling and it was decided to put his racing return back to the following race, at Monza.

He missed his annual outing at his favourite circuit, Spa-Francorchamps, but when he witnessed the massive accidents endured at Eau Rouge by both BAR drivers he must have felt quite glad. First Jacques Villeneuve piled off there in qualifying, miraculously without injury. This stopped the session, but no sooner had it restarted than Ricardo Zonta did likewise, also without injury. But the already financially-stretched BAR team was left reeling with two chassis consigned to the scrap heap.

There were no surprises when Mika Hakkinen took pole, but David Coulthard was hard on his tail and clearly going well. The second row of the grid was all yellow as Heinz-Harald Frentzen was joined by a charged-up Damon Hill who was finally happy with his car. Eddie Irvine lined up sixth.

Coulthard made a better start than Hakkinen and took his line into the first corner. Being a hairpin, there's not much space, but still Hakkinen came on up the inside and they touched. Fortunately for McLaren, this wasn't Austria revisited and both were able to continue on their way. But many in the paddock wondered why McLaren boss Ron Dennis hadn't insisted on team orders in favour of his higher-ranked driver, Hakkinen.

Coulthard put his head down and pulled clear, while Hakkinen ran second ahead of

NO TEAM ORDERS: Mika Hakkinen tries to dive up the inside of David Coulthard at La Source on the opening lap, but he wasn't to find a way by

Frentzen and a fast-starting Irvine. And that is how they ran all the way to the finish, with their order changing only at mid-distance when Ralf Schumacher climbed to third. However, he was running a one-stop strategy and fell back to fifth when his rivals emerged from their second stops. Williams team boss Patrick Head later

accused Ferrari of having Mika Salo block Ralf for several laps after his stop to ensure that the German wouldn't pass Irvine for fourth.

The podium is traditionally a time for good cheer, but there was none issuing from Hakkinen towards Coulthard. But, like it or not, the Scot had beaten him fair and square.

ITALIAN GP

MIKA'S SECOND ITALIAN FLOP

A litany of errors had deprived Mika Hakkinen of points. But he alone was to blame this time for throwing away certain victory when he fell off in Italy for the second time in 1999.

RACE RESULTS

**ROUND 13 AT MONZA,
SEPTEMBER 12, 1999**

53 LAPS—189.87 MILES

	Driver	Team
1	HEINZ-HARALD FRENTZEN	Jordan
2	RALF SCHUMACHER	Williams
3	MIKA SALO	Ferrari
4	RUBENS BARRICHELLO	Stewart
5	DAVID COULTHARD	McLaren
6	EDDIE IRVINE	Ferrari

POLE Mika Hakkinen,
  1m 22.432s (156.59mph/251.99kph)
FASTEST LAP Ralf Schumacher,
  1m 25.579s (150.83mph/242.72kph)
WEATHER Warm, dry and sunny

Arriving at Monza with a lead of just one point over Eddie Irvine wasn't how Mika Hakkinen would have wanted it. Especially as this was after four races in which usual rival Michael Schumacher had been on the sidelines. However, the Finn had the equipment at hand to rectify this and duly planted his Mercedes-engined McLaren on pole for the 11th time.

His advantage was half a second over Jordan's Heinz-Harald Frentzen with David Coulthard third. Much to Mika's frustration, there was still no talk of team orders at McLaren. Fortunately, they were made less imperative as Eddie Irvine was eighth, two slots behind his number two, Mika Salo.

The matter of team orders became irrelevant at the start, when Coulthard found himself edged towards the grass as the fast-starting Alessandro Zanardi made the most of his best grid position – fourth – and Ralf Schumacher also barrelled past.

While the jousting pack fought for position, Hakkinen escaped, with Frentzen also left clear to consolidate his second place as Zanardi led Ralf, Coulthard and Salo, with Irvine not quite able to keep up. And this was how it stayed until Zanardi slowed on lap 18 and waved Ralf through. It seems that his floor had come loose. Before the round of pit stops in this one-stop race, Rubens Barrichello had risen to fifth, the Stewart driver the only one doing any overtaking.

But, shock of shocks, Hakkinen never made it to his pitstop, having spun out at the first chicane when under no pressure. He'd flicked down one gear too many and the rear of his McLaren locked. With the engine stalled, his steering wheel was thrown from the car before it even came to an embarrassing halt. How the *tifosi* bayed their delight and how poor Mika sobbed. This time, there was no-one to blame but himself.

Frentzen found himself as the one with the comfortable lead. It was one that he wasn't to lose either, with Schumacher and Salo joining him on the Monza podium. Barrichello resisted Coulthard's attacks to be fourth, with Irvine amazed to come away with a point in a race where he was convinced that his car's performance was so poor that he would leave Monza empty-handed. So now he was level with Hakkinen at the head of the table.

MISTAKE OF THE YEAR: This moment will haunt Hakkinen for years, as he spun out of the lead when under no pressure

EUROPEAN GP

STEWART SPRINGS A SURPRISE

At the start of the year it looked as though Stewart would become a winning team. At the start of the European GP, it didn't. But through came Johnny Herbert from 14th to take a win.

RACE RESULTS F1

ROUND 14 AT NURBURGRING,
SEPTEMBER 26, 1999

66 LAPS—186.64 MILES

REVIEW OF THE
1999 SEASON

117

Driver	Team
1 JOHNNY HERBERT	Stewart
2 JARNO TRULLI	Prost
3 RUBENS BARRICHELLO	Stewart
4 RALF SCHUMACHER	Williams
5 MIKA HAKKINEN	McLaren
6 MARC GENE	Minardi

POLE Heinz-Harald Frentzen, 1m 19.910s
(127.542mph/205.250kph)
FASTEST LAP Hakkinen, 1m 21.282s
(125.384mph/201.786kph)
WEATHER Cool and overcast then light rain

It's hard to know where to start with the European GP. For all the luck involved, the most important fact is that Stewart achieved the maiden victory that everyone hoped they would before the team is renamed Jaguar Sport.

Good sport should be like good theatre, and it was in qualifying, with suspense maintained to the close. The rain had stopped, but the track remained wet and the best times were set right at the end, with Heinz-Harald Frentzen toppling David Coulthard and Mika Hakkinen. Eddie Irvine ended up ninth.

Come the race, the circuit was dry, but this didn't stop mayhem at the first corner when Damon Hill's Jordan lost power and Alexander Wurz swerved to avoid it, clipping and flipping his Sauber, with Diniz fortunate to escape with bruising from an accident that ripped off his roll-hoop as the car landed inverted.

When the safety car released the field, Frentzen led from Hakkinen, Coulthard, Ralf Schumacher and Giancarlo Fisichella. There was little change, but Irvine was up to fifth by lap 17. And it was at this point that rain started to fall.

Three laps later, Hakkinen was called in for wets, but it failed to become much wetter and he lost a lot of time. He fell to 10th and four laps later came in again for dry tyres. Still, at least they had all his tyres to hand, unlike Ferrari when Irvine pitted…

This left Frentzen and Coulthard out in front. They pitted together on lap 32. They held station as they sprinted out of the pits, but Frentzen slowed at the first corner, left with no power. This left Coulthard clear. And he was pressing on, too. But pressing too hard and he slid off when it started to rain harder, leaving Schumacher with a 20-second lead over

THE SPOILS OF VICTORY: Johnny Herbert, Jackie Stewart and Rubens Barrichello hold up the silverware after Herbert gave the team its first win

Fisichella. However, Schumacher was on a two-stop strategy and his second stop left Fisichella clear, only for the Italian to 'do a Coulthard'.

Schumacher failed to be rewarded, though, as his right rear tyre blew on the very next lap. While he was able to limp back to the pits, this dropped him to fifth place, with Herbert now leading the way from Jarno Trulli, Rubens

Barrichello and Minardi's Luca Badoer.

It wasn't over yet, as Badoer's dream run in the Minardi pulled up short when its gearbox failed. And then Jacques Villeneuve retired from fifth when his clutch failed, elevating Hakkinen to the position after a run in which he appeared to have given up. Minardi at least got something out of the day as Marc Gene grabbed the final point.

MALAYSIAN GP

MALAYSIAN FIREWORKS

RACE RESULTS

ROUND 15 AT SEPANG,
OCTOBER 17, 1999

56 LAPS—192.87 MILES

Pos	Driver	Team
1	EDDIE IRVINE	Ferrari
2	MICHAEL SCHUMACHER	Ferrari
3	MIKA HAKKINEN	McLaren
4	JOHNNY HERBERT	Stewart
5	RUBENS BARRICHELLO	Stewart
6	HEINZ-HARALD FRENTZEN	Jordan

POLE: M Schumacher, 1m39.688s
 (124.372mph/200.148kph)
FASTEST LAP: M Schumacher,
 1m40.267s (123.654mph/198.992kph)
WEATHER: Hot, dry and bright

The World Championship was thrown wide open on its first visit to Sepang. The Ferraris won, then were disqualified, then reinstated, leaving it all to fight for in the Suzuka finale.

Michael Schumacher was back from his six-race absence, to be present for Malaysia's first Grand Prix to support his team-mate Eddie Irvine's World Championship bid. Just a week earlier, Michael had said that he didn't feel ready to drive again. However, one can presume that strong words from the team precipitated his return. Once at Sepang, though, he did everything that could have been asked of him and then some. He qualified on pole by a whisker under a second. Fortunately for Ferrari, Irvine was second, ahead of the McLarens, this time with David Coulthard ahead of Mika Hakkinen.

The tactics were clear, as although Schumacher led Irvine away, he meekly tucked in behind him after three laps and then attempted to ride shotgun and delay the McLarens as much as possible. However, Coulthard silenced the critics who say he can't overtake by diving past Michael for second place a lap later, doing so at Turn 2.

Now, the reason that Coulthard hadn't dropped back to fourth to support Hakkinen's challenge was that he'd started on a light fuel load and it had been decided that his role was to harry Irvine in particular. He duly closed in, but before he could line up the move for the lead that would have altered the course of the race, his fuel pressure dropped and he was out.

So, Hakkinen was left to take on the red cars on his own, and was surely now regretting his choice of the harder compound tyres as he failed to find any way of passing a deliberately slow and obstructive Schumacher.

Irvine duly pitted from the lead, and was still in front when he came in for a second time. But Schumacher was running a one-stop strategy and was in front when Eddie returned. But, true to his word, he pulled over once Hakkinen had pitted for a second time and waved Irvine through to a crucial 10 points. While Schumacher pocketed the six points for second place, Hakkinen had to work hard to claim the four for third, as he'd emerged behind Johnny Herbert's Stewart and only got past when the English driver went wide at Turn 9.

Hours after the race, though, with the bells having been rung around Italy in tribute to Ferrari's perfect result, the stewards ejected both Ferraris for an infringement on their bargeboards. So, instead of Irvine leading Hakkinen to the final race with a four-point advantage, he was now 12 behind and Hakkinen was World Champion for the second year running. And McLaren were Constructors' Cup champions again. However, Ferrari lodged an appeal that was heard in Paris the following Friday and were duly reinstated.

TEAM FORMATION: Ferrari's Schumacher and Irvine salute their one-two

JAPANESE GP

MIKA DOES IT AGAIN

Mika Hakkinen knew that the best way to be sure of retaining his world title was to win at Suzuka. So, that's precisely what he did, with third place not enough for Ferrari's Eddie Irvine.

RACE RESULTS

ROUND 16 AT SUZUKA, OCTOBER 31, 1999

53 LAPS—192.99 MILES

Pos	Driver	Team
1	MIKA HAKKINEN	McLaren
2	MICHAEL SCHUMACHER	Ferrari
3	EDDIE IRVINE	Ferrari
4	HEINZ-HARALD FRENTZEN	Jordan
5	RALF SCHUMACHER	Williams
6	JEAN ALESI	Sauber

POLE M Schumacher, 1m37.470s (134.48mph/216.41kph)
FASTEST LAP M Schumacher, 1m41.319s (129.47mph/208.36kph)
WEATHER Warm, dry and sunny

With Eddie Irvine arriving at Suzuka with a four-point lead over Mika Hakkinen, there were quite a few permutations as to what both drivers had to do to make sure that they were crowned World Champion. They would need the help of their respective teammates David Coulthard and Michael Schumacher. However, Hakkinen felt the best way of clinching his second title was to win the race, as even if Irvine finished second and tied their scores, Hakkinen would be champion thanks to having five wins to Irvine's four.

Schumacher worried Hakkinen by qualifying on pole ahead of the Finn and Coulthard. However, Irvine crashed towards the end of the session and was in fifth. Hakkinen got away cleanly at the start, but Schumacher did not, delaying Coulthard and so the order as they entered the first corner was Hakkinen, Schumacher, Olivier Panis up from sixth on the grid, Irvine and Coulthard. Hakkinen pulled clear and looked as though he would build up a cushion that would allow him an extra pit stop should he want one. Then, with the gap at around nine seconds, Schumacher pegged it.

Panis's promising run for Prost came to naught when his car failed after its first pit stop. This elevated Irvine to third, but crucially Ferrari was out-thought when first Hakkinen came in early for his first pitstop. Then, when Schumacher came in, McLaren realized that Irvine would have to wait another lap and brought Coulthard in from his shadow. Irvine pitted a lap later, but when he rejoined, Coulthard had nipped through to third. Coulthard pulled away to make McLaren look good for the Constructors' Cup as well as the driver's title, but appeared to be instructed to

IT'S ALL OVER: McLaren boss Ron Dennis dishes out his congratulations

drop back and engage Irvine in battle so that Frentzen and Ralf Schumacher could try and pass him. However, when Irvine made an early second stop, Coulthard then tried to pull away again, but clipped a kerb and damaged his car's nose. The delay in changing this took him out of contention. And this was how they stayed to the end, with Hakkinen winning from Schumacher,

and Irvine more than a minute behind his teammate in third but just ahead of Frentzen and Ralf Schumacher, with Jean Alesi rounding out his Sauber career by taking the final point just ahead of the Stewarts.

Ferrari was left with the consolation of winning the Constructors' Cup for the first time since 1983.

NOTE
Drivers are listed according to their finishing position in each race.

SCORING SYSTEM
First, 10 points; second, 6 points; third, 4 points; fourth, 3 points; fifth, 2 points; sixth, 1 point.

	DRIVER	(Nat)	CAR-ENGINE	1 March 7, Melbourne	2 April 11, Interlagos	3 May 2, Imola	4 May 16, Monaco	5 May 30, Barcelona
1	Mika Hakkinen	FIN	McLaren-Mercedes MP4-14	RP	1PF	RP	3PF	1P
2	Eddie Irvine	GBR	Ferrari F399	1	5	R	2	4
3	Heinz-Harald Frentzen	GER	Jordan-Mugen Honda 199	2	3	R	4	R
4	David Coulthard	GBR	McLaren-Mercedes MP4-14	R	R	2	R	2
5	Michael Schumacher	GER	Ferrari F399	8F	2	1F	1	3F
6	Ralf Schumacher	GER	Williams-Supertec FW21	3	4	R	R	5
7	Rubens Barrichello	BRA	Stewart-Ford SF-3	5	R	3	9*	D
8	Johnny Herbert	GBR	Stewart-Ford SF-3	NS	R	10*	R	R
9	Giancarlo Fisichella	ITA	Benetton-Playlife B199	4	R	5	5	9
10	Mika Salo	FIN	BAR-Supertec 01 / Ferrari F399			7*	R	8
11	Damon Hill	GBR	Jordan-Mugen Honda 199	R	R	4	R	7
	Jarno Trulli	ITA	Prost-Peugeot AP02	R	R	R	7	6
13	Pedro Diniz	BRA	Sauber-Petronas C18	R	R	R	R	R
	Alexander Wurz	AUT	Benetton-Playlife B199	R	7	R	6	10
15	Jean Alesi	FRA	Sauber-Petronas C18	R	R	6	R	R
	Olivier Panis	FRA	Prost-Peugeot AP02	R	6	R	R	R
17	Pedro de la Rosa	SPA	Arrows A20	6	R	R	R	11
	Marc Gene	SPA	Minardi-Ford M01	R	9	9	R	R
-	Luca Badoer	ITA	Minardi-Ford M01	R		8	R	R
-	Stephane Sarrazin	FRA	Minardi-Ford M01		R			
-	Toranosuke Takagi	JAP	Arrows A20	7	8	R	R	12
-	Jacques Villeneuve	CAN	BAR-Supertec 01	R	R	R	R	R
-	Alessandro Zanardi	ITA	Williams-Supertec FW21	R	R	11*	8	R
-	Ricardo Zonta	BRA	BAR-Supertec 01	R	NS			

CONSTRUCTOR

				1 March 7, Melbourne	2 April 11, Interlagos	3 May 2, Imola	4 May 16, Monaco	5 May 30, Barcelona
1	Ferrari			10	8	10	16	7
2	McLaren-Mercedes			-	10	6	4	16
3	Jordan-Mugen Honda			6	4	3	3	-
4	Stewart-Ford			2	-	4	-	-
5	Williams-Supertec			4	3	-	-	2
6	Benetton-Playlife			3	-	2	3	-
7	Prost-Peugeot			-	1	-	-	1
8	Sauber-Petronas			-	-	1	-	-
9	Arrows			1	-	-	-	-
	Minardi-Ford							
11	BAR-Supertec							

6 June 13, Montreal	7 June 27, Magny-Cours	8 July 11, Silverstone	9 July 25, A1-Ring	10 August 1, Hockenheim	11 August 15, Hungaroring	12 August 29, Spa-Francorchamps	13 September 12, Monza	14 September 26, Nurburgring	15 October 17, Sepang	16 October 31, Suzuka	Points total
1	2	RPF	3PF	RP	1P	2PF	RP	5F	3	1	76
3F	6	2	1	1	3	4	6	7	1	3	74
11*	1	4	4	3	4	3	1	RP	6	4	54
7	RF	1	2	5F	2F	1	5	R	R	R	48
RP	5	R	-	-	-	-	-	-	2PF	2PF	44
4	4	3	R	4	9	5	2F	4	R	5	35
R	3P	8	R	R	5	10	4	3	5	8	21
5	R	12	14	11*	11	R	R	1	4	7	15
2	R	7	12*	R	R	11	R	R	11	14	13
			9	2	12	7	3	R			10
R	R	5	8	R	6	6	10	R	R	R	7
R	7	9	7	R	8	12	R	2	R	R	7
6	R	6	6	R	R	R	R	R	R	11	3
R	R	10	5	7	7	14	R	R	8	10	3
R	R	14	R	8	16*	9	9	R	7	6	2
9	8	13	10	6	10	13	11	9	R	R	2
R	11	R	R	R	15	R	R	R	R	13	1
8	R	15	11	9	17	16	R	6	9	R	1
10	10	R	13	10	14	R	R	R	R	R	
R	D	16	R	R	R	R	R	R	R	R	
R	R	R	R	R	R	15	8	10	R	9	
R	R	11	R	R	R	8	7	R	10	R	
R	9	R	R	R	13	R	R	8	R	12	

SYMBOLS P denotes pole position; F denotes fastest lap; R denotes retired from race; * denotes classified but not running at finish; NC denotes not classified (ie. still running at the end of the race, but without having covered sufficient distance to be classified); NS denotes did not start the race; NP denotes did not practice; D denotes disqualified; - denotes did not score (In the Constructors' Cup).

6 June 13, Montreal	7 June 27, Magny-Cours	8 July 11, Silverstone	9 July 25, A1-Ring	10 August 1, Hockenheim	11 August 15, Hungaroring	12 August 29, Spa-Francorchamps	13 September 12, Monza	14 September 26, Nurburgring	15 October 17, Sepang	16 October 31, Suzuka	Points total
4	3	6	10	16	4	3	5	-	16	10	128
10	6	10	10	2	16	16	2	2	4	10	124
-	10	5	3	4	4	5	10	-	1	3	61
2	4	-	-	-	2	-	3	14	5	-	36
3	3	4	-	3	-	2	6	3	-	2	35
6	-	-	2	-	-	-	-	-	-	-	16
-	-	-	1	-	-	-	-	6	-	-	9
1	-	1	1	-	-	-	-	-	-	1	5
-	-	-	-	-	-	-	-	-	-	-	1
-	-	-	-	-	-	-	-	1	-	-	1

FORMULA ONE RECORDS

Most Grand Prix starts

DRIVERS

256	Riccardo Patrese (ITA)	145	Johnny Herbert (GBR)
210	Gerhard Berger (AUT)	144	Emerson Fittipaldi (BRA)
208	Andrea de Cesaris (ITA)	135	Jean-Pierre Jarier (FRA)
204	Nelson Piquet (BRA)	132	Eddie Cheever (USA)
199	Alain Prost (FRA)		Clay Regazzoni (SUI)
194	Michele Alboreto (ITA)	128	Mario Andretti (USA)
187	Nigel Mansell (GBR)		Mika Hakkinen (FIN)
176	Graham Hill (GBR)		M Schumacher (GER)
175	Jacques Laffite (FRA)	126	Jack Brabham (AUS)
171	Niki Lauda (AUT)	123	Ronnie Peterson (SWE)
167	Jean Alesi (FRA)	119	Pierluigi Martini (ITA)
163	Thierry Boutsen (BEL)	116	Jacky Ickx (BEL)
161	Ayrton Senna (BRA)		Alan Jones (AUS)
158	Martin Brundle (GBR)	115	Damon Hill (GBR)
152	John Watson (GBR)	114	Keke Rosberg (FIN)
149	Rene Arnoux (FRA)		Patrick Tambay (FRA)
147	Derek Warwick (GBR)	112	Denny Hulme (NZL)
146	Carlos Reutemann (ARG)		Jody Scheckter (RSA)

CONSTRUCTORS

619	Ferrari	394	Brabham	230	March
492	McLaren	375	Prost	197	BRM
490	Lotus	337	Arrows	146	Jordan
418	Tyrrell	283	Benetton	132	Osella
411	Williams	237	Minardi	129	Cooper

THE START OF A RECORD: Patrese began his career with Arrows in 1977 and kept on going until 1992

Most wins

DRIVERS

51	Alain Prost (FRA)		Alan Jones (AUS)
41	Ayrton Senna (BRA)		Carlos Reutemann (ARG)
35	Michael Schumacher (GER)	11	Jacques Villeneuve (CDN)
31	Nigel Mansell (GBR)	10	Gerhard Berger (AUT)
27	Jackie Stewart (GBR)		James Hunt (GBR)
25	Jim Clark (GBR)		Ronnie Peterson (SWE)
	Niki Lauda (AUT)		Jody Scheckter (RSA)
24	Juan Manuel Fangio (ARG)	8	Denny Hulme (NZL)
23	Nelson Piquet (BRA)		Jacky Ickx (BEL)
22	Damon Hill (GBR)	7	Rene Arnoux (FRA)
16	Stirling Moss (GBR)	6	Tony Brooks (GBR)
14	Jack Brabham (AUS)		David Coulthard (GBR)
	Emerson Fittipaldi (BRA)		Jacques Laffite (FRA)
	Mika Hakkinen (FIN)		Riccardo Patrese (FRA)
	Graham Hill (GBR)		Jochen Rindt (AUT)
13	Alberto Ascari (ITA)		John Surtees (GBR)
12	Mario Andretti (USA)		Gilles Villeneuve (CDN)

CONSTRUCTORS

125	Ferrari	15	Renault		Wolf
123	McLaren	10	Alfa Romeo	2	Honda
102	Williams	9	Ligier	1	Eagle
79	Lotus		Maserati		Hesketh
35	Brabham		Matra		Penske
27	Benetton		Mercedes		Porsche
23	Tyrrell		Vanwall		Shadow
17	BRM	3	Jordan		Stewart
16	Cooper		March		

Most wins in one season

DRIVERS

9	Nigel Mansell (GBR) 1992		J Villeneuve (CDN) 1997
	Michael Schumacher (GER) 1995	6	Mario Andretti (USA) 1978
			Alberto Ascari (ITA) 1952
8	Mika Hakkinen (FIN) 1998		Jim Clark (GBR) 1965
	Damon Hill (GBR) 1996		Juan Manuel Fangio (ARG) 1954
	Ayrton Senna (BRA) 1988		
	Michael Schumacher (GER) 1994		Damon Hill (GBR) 1994
			James Hunt (GBR) 1976
7	Jim Clark (GBR) 1963		Nigel Mansell (GBR) 1987
	Alain Prost (FRA) 1984		Michael Schumacher (GER) 1998
	Alain Prost (FRA) 1988		
	Alain Prost (FRA) 1993		Ayrton Senna (BRA) 1989
	Ayrton Senna (BRA) 1991		Ayrton Senna (BRA) 1990

CONSTRUCTORS

15	McLaren 1988	7	Ferrari 1952	Ferrari 1990
12	McLaren 1984		Ferrari 1953	Ferrari 1996
	Williams 1996		Lotus 1963	Ferrari 1998
11	Benetton 1995		Lotus 1973	Ferrari 1999
10	McLaren 1989		McLaren 1999	Lotus 1965
	Williams 1992		Tyrrell 1971	Lotus 1970
	Williams 1993		Williams 1991	Matra 1969
9	McLaren 1998		Williams 1994	McLaren 1976
	Williams 1986	6	Alfa Romeo 1950	McLaren 1985
	Williams 1987		Alfa Romeo 1951	McLaren 1990
8	Benetton 1994		Cooper 1960	Vanwall 1958
	Lotus 1978		Ferrari 1975	Williams 1980
	McLaren 1991		Ferrari 1976	Vanwall 1958
	Williams 1997		Ferrari 1979	Williams 1980

Most consecutive wins

9	Alberto Ascari (ITA) 1952/53	Jochen Rindt (AUT) 1970
5	Jack Brabham (AUS) 1960	Michael Schumacher (GER) 1994
	Jim Clark (GBR) 1965	
	Nigel Mansell (GBR) 1992	Ayrton Senna (BRA) 1988
4	Jack Brabham (AUS) 1966	Ayrton Senna (BRA) 1991
	Jim Clark (GBR) 1963	Jochen Rindt (AUT) 1970
	Juan Manuel Fangio (ARG) 1953/54	Michael Schumacher (GER) 1994
	Damon Hill (GBR) 1995/96	Ayrton Senna (BRA) 1988
	Alain Prost (FRA) 1993	Ayrton Senna (BRA) 1991

Grand Prix starts without a win

208	Andrea de Cesaris (ITA)	113	Rubens Barrichello (BRA)
158	Martin Brundle (GBR)	109	Philippe Alliot (FRA)
147	Derek Warwick (GBR)	97	Chris Amon (NZL)
135	Jean-Pierre Jarier (FRA)	95	Ukyo Katayama (JAP)
132	Eddie Cheever (USA)	93	Ivan Capelli (ITA)
119	Pierluigi Martini (ITA)		

A REGULAR OCCURRENCE: Nigel Mansell became very accustomed to spraying champagne on the podium

Greatest number of fastest laps

DRIVERS

41	Alain Prost (FRA)	19	Damon Hill (GBR)
38	Michael Schumacher (GER)		Ayrton Senna (BRA)
30	Nigel Mansell (GBR)	15	Clay Regazzoni (SUI)
28	Jim Clark (GBR)		Jackie Stewart (GBR)
25	Niki Lauda (AUT)	14	Jacky Ickx (BEL)
23	Juan Manuel Fangio (ARG)	13	Mika Hakkinen (FIN)
	Nelson Piquet (BRA)		Alan Jones (AUS)
21	Gerhard Berger (AUT)		Riccardo Patrese (ITA)
20	Stirling Moss (GBR)	12	Rene Arnoux (FRA)

CONSTRUCTORS

138	Ferrari	20	Tyrrell	12	Matra
111	Williams	18	Renault	11	Ligier
89	McLaren	15	BRM	9	Mercedes
71	Lotus		Maserati	7	March
40	Brabham	14	Alfa Romeo	6	Vanwall
35	Benetton	13	Cooper		

Most pole positions

DRIVERS

65	Ayrton Senna (BRA)	16	Stirling Moss (GBR)
33	Jim Clark (GBR)	14	Alberto Ascari (ITA)
	Alain Prost (FRA)		James Hunt (GBR)
32	Nigel Mansell (GBR)		Ronnie Peterson (SWE)
28	Juan Manuel Fangio (ARG)	13	Jack Brabham (AUS)
24	Niki Lauda (AUT)		Graham Hill (GBR)
	Nelson Piquet (BRA)		Jacky Ickx (BEL)
23	Michael Schumacher (GER)		Jacques Villeneuve (CDN)
21	Mika Hakkinen (FIN)	12	Gerhard Berger (AUT)
20	Damon Hill (GBR)	10	Jochen Rindt (AUT)
18	Mario Andretti (USA)	8	David Coulthard (GBR)
	Rene Arnoux (FRA)		Riccardo Patrese (ITA)
17	Jackie Stewart (GBR)		John Surtees (GBR)

CONSTRUCTORS

127	Ferrari	14	Tyrrell	7	Vanwall
108	Williams	12	Alfa Romeo	5	March
107	Lotus	11	BRM	4	Matra
103	McLaren		Cooper	3	Shadow
39	Brabham	10	Maserati	2	Jordan
31	Renault	9	Ligier		Lancia
16	Benetton	8	Mercedes	1	Stewart

IN ONE SEASON, DRIVERS

14	Nigel Mansell (GBR) 1992		Ronnie Peterson (SWE) 1973
13	Alain Prost (FRA) 1993		Nelson Piquet (BRA) 1984
	Ayrton Senna (BRA) 1988	8	Mario Andretti (USA) 1978
	Ayrton Senna (BRA)1989		James Hunt (GBR) 1976
11	Mika Hakkinen (FIN) 1999		Nigel Mansell (GBR) 1987
10	Ayrton Senna (BRA) 1990		Ayrton Senna (BRA) 1986
	J Villeneuve (CDN) 1997		Ayrton Senna (BRA) 1991
9	Mika Hakkinen (FIN) 1998	7	Mario Andretti (USA) 1977
	Damon Hill (GBR) 1996		Jim Clark (GBR) 1963
	Niki Lauda (AUT) 1974		Ayrton Senna (BRA) 1985
	Niki Lauda (AUT) 1975		

IN ONE SEASON, CONSTRUCTORS

15	McLaren 1988		Williams 1996
	McLaren 1989	11	McLaren 1999
	Williams 1992		Williams 1997
	Williams 1993	10	Ferrari 1974
12	Lotus 1978		Lotus 1973
	McLaren 1990		McLaren 1991
	McLaren 1998		Renault 1982
	Williams 1987	9	Brabham 1984
	Williams 1995		Ferrari 1975

AN ALL-TIME GREAT: Ayrton Senna did almost all his winning with McLaren, claiming three titles

Most championship points

(this figure is gross tally, ie. including scores that were later dropped)

DRIVERS

798.5	Alain Prost (FRA)	294	Mika Hakkinen (FIN)
614	Ayrton Senna (BRA)	289	Graham Hill (GBR)
570	Michael Schumacher (GER)	281	Emerson Fittipaldi (BRA)
			Riccardo Patrese (ITA)
485.5	Nelson Piquet (BRA)	277.5	Juan Manuel Fangio (ARG)
482	Nigel Mansell (GBR)		
420.5	Niki Lauda (AUT)	274	Jim Clark (GBR)
385	Gerhard Berger (AUT)	261	Jack Brabham (AUS)
360	Damon Hill (GBR)	255	Jody Scheckter (RSA)
	Jackie Stewart (GBR)	248	Denny Hulme (NZL)
310	Carlos Reutemann (ARG)	236	Jean Alesi (FRA)

CONSTRUCTORS

2354.5	Ferrari	439	BRM	156	Matra
2324.5	McLaren	420	Prost	84	Sauber
1995.5	Williams	333	Cooper	79	Wolf
1352	Lotus	312	Renault	67.5	Shadow
854	Brabham	216	Jordan	57	Vanwall
847.5	Benetton	171.5	March		
617	Tyrrell	157	Arrows		

GOLDEN BEGINNING: Alain Prost scored the first of his 51 wins with Renault, but won his titles elsewhere

Most drivers titles

5	Juan Manuel Fangio (ARG)	Giuseppe Farina (ITA)
4	Alain Prost (FRA)	Mike Hawthorn (GBR)
3	Jack Brabham (AUS)	Damon Hill (GBR)
	Niki Lauda (AUT)	Phil Hill (USA)
	Nelson Piquet (BRA)	Denis Hulme (NZL)
	Ayrton Senna (BRA)	James Hunt (GBR)
	Jackie Stewart (GBR)	Alan Jones (AUS)
2	Alberto Ascari (ITA)	Nigel Mansell (GBR)
	Jim Clark (GBR)	Jochen Rindt (AUT)
	Emerson Fittipaldi (BRA)	Keke Rosberg (FIN)
	Mika Hakkinen (GFIN)	Jody Scheckter (ZA)
	Graham Hill (GBR)	John Surtees (GBR)
	Michael Schumacher (GER)	Jacques Villeneuve (CDN)
1	Mario Andretti (USA)	

Most constructors titles

9	Ferrari	2	Brabham		Matra
	Williams		Cooper		Tyrrell
8	McLaren	1	Benetton		Vanwall
7	Lotus		BRM		

2000 FIA FORMULA ONE

				March 12, Australian GP	March 26, Brazilian GP	April 9, San Marino GP	April 23, British GP	May 7, Spanish GP	May 21, European GP	June 4, Monaco GP	
1	McLaren	Mika Hakkinen	(FIN)								
2	McLaren	David Coulthard	(GBR)								
3	Ferrari	Michael Schumacher	(GER)								
4	Ferrari	Rubens Barrichello	(BRA)								
5	Jordan	Heinz-Harald Frentzen	(GER)								
6	Jordan	Jarno Trulli	(ITA)								
7	Jaguar	Eddie Irvine	(GBR)								
8	Jaguar	Johnny Herbert	(GBR)								
9	Williams	Ralf Schumacher	(GER)								
10	Williams	Jorg Muller	(GER)								
11	Benetton	Giancarlo Fisichella	(ITA)								
12	Benetton	Alexander Wurz	(AUT)								
14	Prost	Jean Alesi	(FRA)								
15	Prost	Nick Heidfeld	(GER)								
16	Sauber	Pedro Diniz	(BRA)								
17	Sauber	Mika Salo	(FIN)								
18	Arrows	Pedro de la Rosa	(SPA)								
19	Arrows	Toranosuke Takagi	(JAP)								
20	Minardi	Marc Gene	(SPA)								
21	Minardi	Norberto Fontana	(ARG)								
22	BAR	Jacques Villeneuve	(CDN)								
23	BAR	Ricardo Zonta	(BRA)								

WORLD CHAMPIONSHIP

2000 FIA FORMULA ONE WORLD CHAMPIONSHIP

127

June 18, Canadian GP	July 2, French GP	July 16, Austrian GP	July 30 German GP	August 13, Hungarian GP	August 27, Belgian GP	September 10, Italian GP	September 24, United States GP	October 8, Japanese GP	October 22, Malaysian GP

RECOGNISING YOUR ENEMY: Mika Hakkinen glances across at his longtime arch-rival Michael Schumacher

The publishers would like to thank the following sources for their kind permission to reproduce the pictures in this book:

Allsport UK Ltd 20, 23/Stanley Chou 98, Michael Cooper 19, 21, 24, 31, 34, 37, 39, 42, 48, 54, 78, 85, 86, 88, 92, 93, 102, 102, 102-3, 103, 105, 108, 112, 116, 117, 118, 128, Craig Jones 94, 95, Jean-Marc Loubat 5, 68, 96, Clive Mason 113, Pascal Rondeau 40, 67, 97, 124, Mark Thompson 2-3, 4, 26, 32, 35, 51, 75, 76,79.

Empics 12, 27, 28, 29, 44, 47, 99, 107,119.

LAT Photographic 55, 64-5, 111, 114, 122/Lorenzo Bellanca 59, 73, Charles Coates 10-1, 18, 59, 70, 71, 74, 80, 83, 91, 103, Malcoln Griffiths 81, Gavin Lawrence 57, 82, 89, 110, M. Levitt 56, M. Steven Tee 5, 8-9, 15, 66, 72, 100-1, 106, 109.
ITV Network 8.
Sporting Pictures (UK) Ltd 4, 6-7, 13, 14, 16, 17, 22, 25, 30, 33, 36, 38, 41, 43, 45, 46, 49, 50, 52, 53, 69, 77, 84, 87, 90, 102, 104, 115, 123, 125.

Every effort has been made to acknowledge correctly and contact the source and/copyright holder of each picture, and Carlton Books Limited apologises for any unintentional errors or omissions which will be corrected in future editions of this book.